SEEMING, BEING AND BECOMING
ACTING IN OUR CENTURY

SEEMING, BEING AND BECOMING

ACTING IN OUR CENTURY

Robert L. Benedetti

Illustrations by the author

Calligraphy by Barbara Wampole

Symbology from
The Taoist and Tantric traditions

Drama Book Specialists (Publishers)
New York

Library of Congress Cataloging in Publication Data

Benedetti, Robert L
    Seeming, being, and becoming.

    Bibliography: p.
    1. Acting.   I. Title.
PN2061.B394   792'.028   76-26668
ISBN 0-910482-77-2 Cloth
ISBN 0-89676-011-1 Paper
10 9 8 7 6 5 4 3 2

Printed in the United States of America

To Joseph Chaikin—
One of those
who has never done
anyone's work but his own.

Contents

Introduction

My first book, *The Actor at Work*, was written six years ago and was premised upon the belief that the art of acting involves three basic skills: (1) mastery of the materials of acting—the self, the partner, the space and the text; (2) physical and vocal freedom of expression; and (3) the mysterious *mimetic* ability to play a role, to express one's own human vitality in a new form—in short, to undergo transformation. I called these three fundamental skills *analytical, expressive* and *spiritual*.

The Actor at Work was addressed to the first two kinds of skills, the analytical and the expressive. I hoped that these formal techniques could serve as the discipline whereby that third "unteachable" spiritual skill could be developed. The oriental actor, for example, uses his physical training as the mechanism of a spiritual discipline in much the way that most eastern religions involve a bodily regimen; I believed that the western actor could use his technique in the same way, if it became as strong and complete (in its own way) as that of the Asian actor. My experience in the last six years has confirmed this belief.

But I have also realized that we western actors don't focus enough of our work on the spiritual objectives of our theatre, and that we could do much more to find a sense of our own theatrical purpose in deeply human terms. I find today's young actors ravenous for a sense of the spiritual potential of the theatre and today's theatre desperate with the need for spiritual revivification.

1

Seeming, Being and Becoming

Regrettably, we have little sense of the wholeness of our theatrical tradition and thus little confidence in the importance of acting specifically within our culture and generally within the total human situation. It is therefore to the perception of acting as a *necessary spiritual enterprise* that this discussion is dedicated.

Insofar as the living actor is at the center of any theatre, what is said here treats not only the actor but also the theatre itself. It is written from a completely personal point of view and is designed to *stimulate* rather than to *persuade*, to excite an examination of fundamental values which the reader must then pursue in his own way.

The discussion is organized into three parts: the first examines the human needs which, in any time, give real purpose to the art of acting; the second traces the development of one contemporary idea of acting through representative twentieth-century figures (Stanislavski, Meyerhold, Brecht, Artaud, Grotowski, and the Living Theatre); the last part is a notebook which, in the way of a mosaic, is my conjecture on the state and future of the actor.

The five years which have passed since this book was conceived have seen many changes in our theatre which confirm the sense of rebirth expressed here. Increasing numbers of young persons are entering serious training and working situations with a degree of artistic and ethical commitment which has rarely been equaled in our history. The growth of theatre on all levels—commercial, academic, community, and avant-garde—is enormous.

Many of the practicing theatre artists discussed here have extended their work into further forms, especially the Becks; others have entered entirely new phases of work, as has Grotowski. In these cases, my comments must be understood within the perspective of the time of my writing. Still other artists, only mentioned in passing here, have assumed positions of mature leadership. Certainly my brief history of acting in our century would now need to include Joseph Chaikin's Open Theater, Richard Schechner's Performance Group, André Gregory's Manhattan Project, The Iowa Theatre Laboratory, The Magic Theatre of Omaha and many others.

Part One
Roots

Roots gather nourishment for the plant
Give it stability
They account for much of its mass
But are largely invisible

There was a time in the sixties when many of us feared for the very existence of the live theatre. The great dream of the fifties for the widespread growth of repertory theatres and their impact on the training of actors and the development of new plays had come crashing down; many of our fine young artists were deserting the live stage for media careers, and even those who remained faithful to their roots were despondent.

From the perspective of the mid-seventies, however, we can see that this was only a passing period of despair and that a process of rebirth has already begun. Not only are "alternative" theatres flourishing, but the mainstream of the traditional theatre has begun to flow vigorously in new directions. It is as if the theatre had seemed to die only in order to pass into a new incarnation; we are lucky enough to be living during the time of its rebirth and reformation.

The traditional theatre has been forced to re-examine itself—in fact to justify itself—by several hard facts. First, traditional theatre has become extremely expensive; as the cost-per-unit of most things in our culture drops through technological advances, the cost of the performing arts (since they cannot be mass produced) appears to double every ten years or so.[1] Either theatre must change its present unwieldy form or no one but the government will be able to afford it by the year 2000.

[1] See William J. Baumol and William G. Bowen, *Performing Arts: The Economic Dilemma* (New York: Twentieth Century Fund, 1966).

Seeming, Being and Becoming

Secondly, the live stage has been challenged by mechanical media which do some things better: film and TV have a scenic flexibility and an ability to manipulate the spectator's point of view which gives them a range of effects previously impossible in even the most elaborate theatres. Moreover, the camera has the ability to focus on detail and give us a proximity to the actor which, in skilled hands, can provide experiences of great subtlety and power.

By themselves, however, these real economic and aesthetic challenges cannot entirely account for the decline of live theatre. The theatre has always competed with other forms of entertainment for its audience—in the past with bear-baiting, the circus or athletics—and it has also always been more expensive to produce than most of the other arts. No, our culture could certainly support and afford the theatre if it wished: the U.S. government spends more on poison gas than it does on theatre, and even the artistically enlightened Canadians spend more on military bands than they do on all of the performing arts.

The real problem is not the complexity or cost of theatre, nor the competition from other forms of entertainment which it faces: the crucial fact is that people in general don't much *like* to go to the theatre, nor have they any sense of the *real needs* which the theatre might fulfill for them. Going to the theatre has always required of the spectator an investment of time, energy and money; people stopped going when they felt that the investment was not being repaid with interest. The theatre has been thus forced to re-examine itself, like many of our other social institutions.

In this re-examination, the theatre has begun to search for the unique quality of experience which it can offer and which cannot be duplicated by any other art or activity. Time after time, one answer has emerged, one crucial element which no other media possesses: *the living presence of the actor.* Whatever new forms theatre may take, it is clear that the living actor will continue to be at the center of the theatre of the future.

The most crucial experimental work of the past century of theatre, regardless of its form or philosophy, has therefore centered upon the actor. We are learning more about him, about the various ways in which he can function and the kinds of skills he can employ. We have the advantage of new concepts and techniques borrowed from other arts and sciences to help us in our examination of the acting process.

Most importantly, we are finally asking not only *what* and *how* the actor is, but also *who* and *why* he is. If the actor is at the center of the theatre, we want to know what is at the center of the actor; we sense that it is somehow here, at the level of the actor's own humanity and the way in which his humanity can relate to the humanity of the spectator, that the real power, beauty and justification for theatre is to be found.

As a result, the direction of theatre in our century has been toward a growing sense of the human immediacy of the art, and we have begun to value the uniquely *spiritual* experiences which can pass between actor and spectator. I use the term "spiritual," depleted and cheapened as it has come to be, not in any dogmatic or even theistic way, but rather to describe the potential of the living theatrical event to celebrate and extend the mutuality of human experience by heightening our sense of immediate aliveness. It is this savoring of the fullness of human encounter and the unique magnetism of the communal spectacle which no mechanical medium, however subtle, can possibly duplicate.

This new emphasis has in no way been restricted to the avant-garde: we have begun to see its effect in the most conservative kinds of theatre. Even Broadway has undergone what might be called a spiritual revival, however shallow, undisciplined and hypocritical the early forms of commercial beatification were. I believe that the meretricious novelty of these first productions having passed, the theatre, in all its aspects, has begun to pursue a serious and unpretentious spirituality.

The way toward this theatrical spirituality is being led by those most involved with the reform of acting, those who most wish to make the degraded art of the actor once again aesthetically significant and ethical. Many of these innovators have begun to re-examine the origins of the actor in search of renewed inspiration, for we feel that our theatre has somehow lost a seriousness and a spirituality with which it began in ancient times.

Ideas about the genesis of the actor are necessarily conjectural; the actor's art produces a completely ephemeral and subjective experience at a given moment in time and is therefore impossible to record. Even films of stage performances fail utterly to communicate the essential subjective essence of the original moment, making the recent past of the actor almost as obscure to us as his distant past.

Seeming, Being and Becoming

Only a few "objective" facts about the actor's origin have won general although tentative agreement. We think that western acting began around 534 B.C. when an actor named Thespis won the first tragic contest; this occasion marked the emergence of the actor as an individual performer from the earlier choric contests in which the Greeks sponsored groups of men and boys who recited poetry in competition with groups from other tribes. Gradually, according to this theory, a solo speaker began to stand apart from the chorus and as he began to adopt a specific role or character, he became the prototype of the actor. From this beginning more actors were added, and after a very long time the chorus eventually disappeared, at least in most plays.

This convenient and interesting theory unfortunately tells us very little of any significance about the reasons for the emergence of the actor: *why* did all this happen? Actors—and here I include such itinerant and "vulgar" traditions as the traveling comedians, medicine men, minstrels, geeks, clowns and all the other circus folk—have been important in every Western culture, however "primitive" or "sophisticated" (themselves meaningless terms in relation to theatre). Surely there is some fundamental human need or conspiracy of needs which gives rise to all this acting.

The following discussion examines some of the ways in which acting has its roots in a variety of basic human needs. No one of these roots is by itself the source of acting, of course, but together they conspire to motivate the existence of live theatre in its multiplicity of forms.

One of the oldest and deepest roots of the actor, one which he shares with the athlete and the dancer, relates to the sheer physical virtuosity of the performer. On this most basic physical level we may view acting as a celebration of potency—potency of the individual human being, of the race and of nature itself.

Acting as a Celebration of Potency

Ancient man did not assume that the yearly renewal of the life-cycle with the coming of spring was inevitable, nor did he assume that the earth would bring forth an abundant harvest; rather, he regarded each new year's growing season as a temporary lease which he attempted to renew annually through a variety of sacrifices and rituals. When the renewal did indeed make itself manifest, and when the harvest was successful, these were occasions for great celebrations, and still are.

The ancient Greek dramatic festivals were such seasonal celebrations. The cycle of the seasons, then, with its hopefully unending sequence of decay and rebirth, was a central rhythm in the genesis of the ancient drama.

On a personal level, each individual's hope for potency—in rites of puberty and of mating—was likewise a source of numerous rituals and celebrations. Such rituals persist today in the Bar Mitzvah, the throwing of rice at weddings, baby showers and in many other practices. Just as the renewal of nature's potency through the cycle of the seasons was the "metaphysical" root of ancient drama, then, the individual's ability to transform *himself*, to summon forth from himself new life as does the coming of spring from the barren winter earth, was its personal, individualistic aspect. No artist sums up man's potential for personal renewal better than does the actor, who summons from himself a new identity, a new level of reality and experience, with each role he creates. So while the cycle of the seasons was the central rhythm

9

of the ancient drama, the actor's ability to transform *himself* was its central image and process.

The celebration of potency of the natural order and of individual man is expressed in one of the oldest known dramatic rituals, the four-thousand-year-old Memphite Drama of Egypt. This yearly spring celebration centered around the legend of Osiris, who was perhaps an early personification of the god of the theatre, Dionysus. According to the legend, Osiris, god of the River Nile and its valley, was murdered by his jealous brother Set, lord of the surrounding desert. To prevent the possible resurrection of Osiris by his many friends and worshipers, Set cut the body of Osiris into pieces and scattered them throughout the kingdom. Despite Set's precautions, however, Osiris' widow, Isis, collected the parts of the corpse and eventually was able to restore Osiris to life.

This myth symbolizes the power of the fertile Nile valley to come to new life each spring as the blood-red river rises to embrace the seed lying within the barren earth. The ancient Egyptians celebrated this yearly renewal of life with a protracted ritual in a quasi-dramatic form: each spring the Pharaoh traveled through the kingdom retracing the journey of Isis, performing a segment of the ritual at the resting place of each part of Osiris' body. The Pharaoh's journey culminated in the great phallic festival of the Pamylea which celebrated the final resurrection. While this ritual was not strictly speaking a drama and the Pharaoh was not exactly an actor, this celebration did express the same process which was at work in the later evolution of theatrical form: *an event of cosmic and personal significance symbolically re-enacted by a celebrant.*

Notice that this ritual served not only a celebratory function, but also subjected the Pharaoh to a yearly test of his individual potency; moreover, his physical stamina, proven by his ordeal, was not only a test of his strength to govern, but also a symbolic affirmation of the potency of his entire culture. We see the same impulse at work in the many modern religious and governmental practices which require periodic pilgrimages or prolonged public ceremonies by the leader.

The art of the actor involves something of this same affirmation of physical potency. Just as we admire the athlete or dancer and enjoy feeling in our own bodies something of their freedom and mastery, we may also enjoy the physical virtuosity of the actor. The clearest demonstration of this is the actor-athlete of the

Chinese tradition, and it is no accident that he has become the model for most contemporary western acting theory.

The particularly physical nature of theatre in all cultures, however, has always required bodily virtuosity of the actor, in whatever form this may have been required at various times in the theatre's history. Although only a few of today's actors can boast of extraordinary physical or vocal abilities, we must remember that the dominantly realistic theatre of the past seventy years tended to de-emphasize such skills.

The importance of physical virtuosity is becoming stronger each day in today's theatre and we are beginning to realize that through his mastery the actor may serve as an example and celebration of physical and spiritual excellence for our culture, as he has done for centuries in the Asian theatre.

The various celebrations of potency we have discussed were more than expressions of gratitude and delight; they were also ways of encouraging the miracle of rebirth to occur by pleasing the gods and creating favorable circumstances. Thus, we must also view one of the impulses behind acting as a kind of sympathetic magic.

Acting as
Sympathetic Magic

Ancient man, depending on events beyond his immediate control (such as needed rain, a good harvest or a successful hunt), attempted to encourage these events to occur by "symbolically" enacting them. The actor-priests who became the figures of the enacted myth were not only celebrating, but also invoking the powers of the gods and thereby attempting through magic to extend their own limited human capabilities.

Imagine a hungry tribe around a fire, hoping for the appearance of game; someone gets up and begins acting like an elephant, someone else enacts the part of the hunter who stalks and kills it. This simple drama with its rudimentary actors is a signal to the gods, an externalization and objectification of the inner desires and needs of the tribe. Repeated by generation after generation, the story is extended and specified; the hunter takes on a personalized character; eventually the story is conventionalized, projected onto a cosmic level, and becomes a *myth*.

Such myths or legends were expressions of underlying recurrent patterns of human experience, objectified, personified and projected by man onto the cosmos. These myths became the substance of a great anthropomorphic drama which served ancient man as a metaphysics (explaining the origins of life and the operation of natural order) and as a psychology (explaining something of the workings of the human soul). These myths, being essentially dramatic in form, lent themselves to increasingly formal and complete theatricalization.

13

Seeming, Being and Becoming

The practice of mythic enactment is not limited to tribal socie-
ties nor has it been abandoned by our own culture; many of our
important undertakings (war, marriage, graduation, birth and
death) involve a wide spectrum of festivals, political ceremonies
and traditional observances which are actually elaborate rituals
whose real purpose is to help insure the success of the venture. We
may see such rituals, primitive or sophisticated, ancient or contemporary, as one of the sources of theatre, if not an incipient
form of theatre itself.

Many traditional aesthetic theorists would argue, however, that
before such theatricalized rituals can be called theatre itself, they
must be transformed from simply utilitarian practices into "art."
This occurs, these critics argue, when the ritual is cut loose from
its utilitarian objective and takes on a life and purpose of its own;
the rain dance, for example, once performed in order to encourage
rain, becomes "art" when it is performed not to bring rain but *for its
own sake* as a beautiful or enjoyable act.

This idea of "art for its own sake" and not for any practical
purpose is part of the aesthetic heritage left us by the nineteenth
century. Oscar Wilde summed it up:

> We can forgive a man for making a useful thing,
> as long as he does not admire it. The only
> excuse for making a useless thing is that one
> admires it intensely. All art is quite useless.[2]

Most present day art, however, has rejected this nineteenth-
century notion of non-utilitarianism and is returning to a sense of
art which is motivated by specific and practical objectives. In the
contemporary theatre, these objectives may be expressed in political, therapeutic or spiritual terms, but whatever their form they
represent *useful* theatre which attempts to bring about real results
in the form of a practical effect upon the spectator.

This useful theatre is itself premised upon the operation of sympathetic magic. Just as ancient man hoped that the enactment of
the myth would "sympathetically" encourage good fortune, so too
the contemporary theatre assumes that the theatrical performance can sympathetically bring about a real effect in the on-
looker. The fundamental assumption of most contemporary theatre, in fact, is that *the condition of the actor is to some degree recreated*

---

[2] *The Picture of Dorian Grey* (Harmondsworth, England: Penguin Books, 1963), p. 5.

14

sympathetically in the spectator and that the spectator's condition may therefore be altered by this experience.

This idea is not too different from the operation of "catharsis" which Aristotle described as having occurred in the ancient Greek drama. In his view the actor's performance excited in the audience the tragic emotions of pity and fear. This experience of pity for the character (and fear for ourselves were we actually in his place) moves us so deeply that our own real emotions become involved. This provides us with a release or *purgation* of potentially injurious tensions which we have carried into the theatre from real life, so that we leave the theatre cleansed and ready to live more fruitfully. Aristotle explains that this phenomenon is premised upon the spectator's fellow-feeling or *sympathaeia* for the performed character; because we feel ourselves to be "like" the hero, we undergo something of his experience. This purgation is obtained, in short, by the kind of sympathetic magic between actor and spectator which is today commonly called *empathy* or *in-feeling*.

So, although today's theatrical rituals are not expected to work magic in the sense of causing rain or a successful hunt, they are increasingly designed to produce real effects on the individual personality of the spectator in much the way that the ancient ritual was meant to celebrate and extend the worshiper's own human vitality. The contemporary theatre is returning to a sense of such "magical acts," and the actor is returning to his ancient role of magician and celebrant.

Acting as Transformation

The Greek play festivals were "gifts" to Dionysus, a very old god whose roots probably go back at least four thousand years to Egypt's Osiris or beyond. Dionysus was also commonly called Bacchus, and we commonly associate him with the "orgies" of Bacchic revelry. It is in the nature of this ancient god, who is still worshiped today, that the deepest impulses motivating the theatre and the actor may be found, for this god of the theatre is himself an actor and a lover of disguise, trickery and transformation. He is the god of potency—of the ecstatic, irrational and sexual vitality—which moves men as a race through time.

The development of theatre was closely involved with the worship of Dionysus, and both depended upon the phenomenon of *transformation*, man's ability to transcend the limits of ordinary existence and enter into new states of being, into extended or even separate realities. The Bacchic reveler, through wine and the frenzy of exhaustion, entered into states of expanded consciousness similar to those produced today by drugs or meditative disciplines; his worship usually took the form of a *masked dance*, with Dionysus himself most commonly represented by the mask of a bull. Indeed, the masked dance, like that of the Bacchic revels, is regarded by some as the true origin of the actor.

The mask, ancient and mysterious, is strongly associated with Dionysus and the other personas (Bacchus, Pan, etc.) which he has assumed. It is also a feature of most tribal rituals and celebrations in other cultures, from the African medicine man to the Kachinas of the American Hopi Indians. The wearing of masks seems to have been a way for man in many cultures and eras to experience something of divinity and immortality for, by donning the mask of the god, the worshiper becomes "possessed" by the god. The importance of the mask, therefore, is that it carries a vitality of its own, derived both from the mythic being it represents and from its ability to excite belief in the wearer and his audience.

> . . . (T)he mask in a primitive festival is revered
> and experienced as a veritable apparition of the
> mythical being that it represents—even though
> everyone knows that a man made the mask and
> that a man is wearing it. The one wearing it,
> furthermore, is identified with the god during the
> time of the ritual of which the mask is part. He
> does not merely represent the god; he *is* the god.[3]

The mask, with its mythic vitality, seizes its mortal wearer, producing a metaphorical combination of transitory human energy vitalizing an eternal form, of *mortal* energies activating an *immortal* form. As Walter Otto puts it in his study of Dionysus:

> . . . the primal phenomenon of duality, the
> incarnate presence of that which is remote, the
> shattering encounter with the irrevocable, the
> fraternal confluence of life and death.
> This duality has its symbol in the mask.
> The whole spendor of that which has been
> submerged draws imperatively near at the same
> time that it is lost in eternity. The wearer of the
> mask is seized by the sublimity and dignity of
> those who are no more. He is himself and yet
> someone else. Madness has touched him—
> something of the spirit of the dual being who lives
> in the mask and whose most recent descendant is
> the actor.[4]

The wearing of the mask is, in short, a celebration of that irrational vitality from which life itself springs, what Dylan Thomas called "the force that through the green fuse drives the flower." The ebb and flow of this life force, the "fraternal conflu-

---

[3] Joseph Campbell *The Masks of God: Primitive Mythology* (New York: Viking Press, 1959), p. 2.
[4] *Dionysus: Myth and Cult* (Bloomington: Indiana University Press, 1965), p. 210.

ence of life and death," is itself a great drama, the *uberdrama* perhaps, and has always been the central spectacle of great theatre. The actor's ability to transform himself, to be "himself and yet someone else," is a testament to the continual cycle of life and the dynamism of life-energy which manifests itself only through continual change. From the actor's point of view, the concept of the mask must be understood in a very broad sense: a mask, or the principle of maskness, is *any object or pattern of behavior which is designed to project a sense of the self.* Persona is the ancient word for mask, and it is the root from which we derive the word *personality.* Your personality is itself a mask, a pattern of behavior whereby you present a sense of yourself to your world.

Acting is based upon this everyday life-principle, with important extensions and modifications. In real life you perform sets of actions which become a mask presented to others, and your social audience responds to this mask as if it were your authentic "self"; if I convince you that I am a certain kind of person, it is not necessarily because I am that person, but because I have performed my mask of actions successfully. Social psychologist Erving Goffman explains it this way:

> In our society the character one performs and
> one's self are somewhat equated. A correctly
> staged and performed scene leads the audience to
> impute a self to a performed character, but this
> imputation—this self—is a *product* of a scene that
> comes off, and is not a *cause* of it. The self, then,
> as a performed character, is not an organic thing
> that has a specific location, whose fundamental
> fate is to be born, to mature, and to die; it is a
> dramatic effect arising diffusely from a scene that
> is presented. . . .[5]

For the ancient worshiper or actor, the mask was a literal, tangible object to be worn, which carried with it a vitality of its own. The contemporary actor rarely wears a literal mask, but he still creates *a pattern of actions* which projects a sense of persona. This pattern of actions becomes the "mask" of the created character; since the sensitive actor responds to the life of his character as

[5] *The Presentation of Self in Everyday Life* (Garden City, N.Y.: Doubleday, 1959), pp. 254-55.

having a vitality of its own, his attitude toward his *mask of actions* remains very much like the one his ancient predecessor assumed toward his literal mask.

When the mask-wearer dons his mask, then, he is literally *impersonating* in the root sense of that word: *im-persona, going into a new mask.* He is *trans-forming* himself, *going into a new mask form,* and we who watch project onto his new form a sense of new identity which, in fact, is a projection of *our own* consciousness into the new form suggested by his performance. It is our belief in the mask which permits it to seem truly alive or authentic; in this way the actor's transformation becomes the occasion for a "sympathetic" transformation by the spectator in his own terms.

For our purposes, then, we may define an actor as *someone who disciplines himself to enter into a new persona through his theatrical craft.* The range of performers who fall into this category include clowns and some other circus folk, storytellers, some comedians and dancers as well as traditional stage and media actors; they all *impersonate* in some way. Many regard this to be the main reason why people become actors; here are four such views of the actor's fine madness:

PETER BROOK: I've had the feeling year after year in working with and talking to and knowing actors that most actors, in a sort of classic, clinical, casebook way, at the age of ten have wished to write off the nature and personality that they were born with, and have found in play-acting a perfect way of life by which they can act out fantasies that they prefer to their own lives, in which they can disguise themselves day after day . . . and the notion that on the stage, in a theatre, you take on a different identity is the very reason that they wish to go into this career.

TYRONE GUTHRIE: I think there probably is something neurotic about wanting to go on the stage, just as there is something even more neurotic about wanting to go into the Church, or into plumbing, or onto the stock market. But I do not think actors go on stage primarily to exhibit themselves, to show off. The profession does involve quite a lot of exhibitionism and showing off, but it also involves a great deal of hiding behind the personality of the character you are pretending to be. And most of the best actors, in my opinion, do their best when there's a good deal to hide behind in the way of all sorts of characteristics in the character and all sorts of hidey things in the makeup—beards, false stomachs, bandy legs, all that kind of thing—and part of the pleasure for the actor, I think, is being somebody who looks and sounds and feels quite different from your dreary old self.

GEORGE C. SCOTT: I think you have to be schizoid three different ways to be an actor. You've got to be three different people: you have to be a human being, then you have to be the character you're playing, and on top of that you've got to be the guy sitting out there in row 10, watching yourself and judging yourself. That's why most of us are crazy to start with or go nuts once we get into it. I mean, don't you think it's a pretty spooky way to earn a living?

MICHAEL GREEN: Perhaps it all starts at school, where in a mustache made from burnt cork the trembling infant actor is pushed reluctantly on stage to mouth his halting lines while the child playing opposite bursts into tears for some unspecified reason. It is then that he discovers, execrable though he may be, that for the first time in his life several hundred people are actually paying attention to him. It is too much for the immature mind.[6]

The stage actor's ability to transform himself has, in the past century, been generally defined in terms of the appearances of ordinary reality. Most of our recent acting techniques have been devoted to a replication of "true-to-life" reality in the sense of impersonating everyday characters. Today's actor, however, is reaching out into new forms, trying to give his audience not only insight into the ordinary but also experiences of nonordinary, extended and even separate realities. Nevertheless, the fundamental process of acting still involves a special kind of impersonation and this process must be understood in a very specific way.

[6] Brook, Guthrie and Scott quoted in news interviews; Green from *Downwind of Upstage* (New York: Hawthorn Books, 1964), pp. 14-15.

Acting as Impersonation

With the coming of spring, the Eskimo who have lived the long winter in separate family-size igloos connect their houses with passageways and gather as a community for an extended festival. One of their celebrations is a masked dance in which various members of the tribe are humorously caricatured. Perhaps the hostilities and frustrations harbored over the long, confined winter are harmlessly released in this dance; as Aristotle pointed out, one function of comedy is to render the dangerous harmless by releasing them in laughter. In any case, man in his many cultures has always found some deep satisfaction in the impersonation of others. In our theatrical tradition the impersonation of specific persons for both comic and tragic purposes is as old as the drama itself. We continue to see it even in our contemporary theatre: Luther, Becket, F.D.R., Dylan Thomas, Brendan Behan, Adolf Eichmann, Pope Pius XII, Chief Joseph, Christ, the Chicago Seven and Lenny Bruce are only a few subjects of recent theatrical impersonations.

Impersonation, however, must be understood in a broader, more useful sense than merely as the replication of another's appearance. For example, the last decade featured a number of one-man shows in which an actor impersonated a famous figure: Hal Holbrook as Mark Twain, Max Adrian as Bernard Shaw, Emlyn Williams as Charles Dickens or Dylan Thomas. In none of these performances did the actor merely "look like" his subject in the literal sense; the actor's genius was expressed by going beyond (and beneath) literal appearances to create an experience which captured the *spirit* of the subject and, moreover, *captured it in a way that revealed some more universal human truth*. It is never enough for the actor merely to put on a convincing mask, to merely *seem* to be someone else; he must wear the mask of his character in such a way that he creates a new and meaningful reality with its own deeper truth in the process.

Furthermore, unlike the examples of specific impersonations noted above, characters in most plays are not "real" by the standards of everyday life, nor is the world of most plays premised upon ordinary reality. Reality may take many forms in the theatre, and each must be respected in its own terms—each may offer us its own kind of truth.

The process of impersonation remains essentially unchanged for the actor, whether he represents ordinary reality or enters into heightened, extended or even separate realities. In all cases, the actor's fundamental task is a dual one—that of *seeming* and *being*: no matter how much he *seems* to be someone else by wearing or projecting a new persona, his creation must also have its own reality, it must also *be* in its own right.

All periods in the theatre have achieved their own balance between seeming and being. In some kinds of acting, the actor's own presence is a dominant element in the performance (as was the case with the great "stars" of the nineteenth century and is still the case with our own movie idols). Some kinds of plays, like those of Brecht, even encourage us to see the actor's own face behind the mask of the character. On the other hand, some actors (like Michael Redgrave, for instance) seem nearly faceless until they become their character, and some plays, like those of O'Neill, require the actor to disappear completely behind the opaque mask of his character.

In fact, we can think of the balance between seeming and being as represented by a mask which can be made either transparent or opaque, allowing us to see more or less of the actor's face beneath it. If we now imagine our changeable mask as a set of postures, gestures, sounds and actions performed by the actor, requiring a greater or lesser degree of transformation by him, then we can understand how different kinds of acting, having different pur-poses, require different relationships of actor and character, different balances of seeming and being.

For the actor, this balancing expresses itself as a peculiar kind of dual consciousness. As Fanny Kemble, a great actress of the late nineteenth century, put it:

> The curious part of acting, to me, is the sort of double process which the mind carries on at once, the combined operation of one's faculties, so to speak, in diametrically opposite directions; for instance, in that very last scene of Mrs. Beverley, while I was half dead with crying in the midst of the *real* grief, created by an entirely *unreal* cause, I perceived that my tears were falling like rain all over my silk dress, and spoiling it.[7]

This dual consciousness, of the created character with its own identity existing simultaneously with the actor's personal identity and his theatrical concerns, is similar to the ancient mask-wearer's experience of being "possessed" by his mask. It is a special madness, this "being yourself and yet someone else," and does suggest that acting is a kind of controlled schizophrenia—but it is an important and potentially beautiful kind of madness.

This dual existence is a feature of *all* acting: no matter how opaque the mask required by the play may be, we never entirely lose sight of the actor's own face, nor does the actor lose a sense of his own separate identity; if he did, he would lose aesthetic choice and would turn his "fine madness" into pathological insanity. Nor, on the other hand, is the mask ever so transparent that we lose sight of it either, for even though the actor may momentarily drop his mask and reveal his own face, he *cannot discard his mask altogether.* Without his mask he is not an actor, he is only a man. (The traditional curtain call, for example, is a taking off of the mask to permit the actor to receive our thanks for his skill in his own person.)

It is the mask which carries the vitality of the god, which the wearer may only share. In a very real way, then, it is the *immortality of the mask which helps to define the mortal authenticity of the wearer.* The theatre relies upon the operation of dual consciousness, upon the simultaneous awareness of the actor's face and the mask of the character, to help us to realize that we have the spiritual capability to redefine our own existence and to move from one reality into another.

---

[7] Quoted by William Archer in *Masks or Faces* (New York: Hill & Wang, 1957), p. 185.

Acting and the Oral Tradition

Today the actor's mask is almost never an actual, physical one but rather a pattern of behavior which the actor "puts on" and fills with the energies of true life. This pattern of behavior is, for most of today's actors, suggested by the words of a text and the actions and qualities which these words can communicate. Thus, the written text may best be understood as the source of the contemporary actor's mask; it serves him as a myth once served his ancient prototype.

The conscientious actor uses the text eagerly, letting it excite in him the creation of a performance of which, finally, words are only a part. Thus the actor's interpretive function, far from being an onerous duty, is in fact the most common way in which today's actor assumes his mask. The text, creatively used, is never a limitation on the actor's own identity, but instead can be the mechanism of his transformation and thus of his liberation through magic.

The importance of the text as the source of the actor's mask has recently been much misunderstood. Beginning with Artaud, who derided the "dictatorship of speech" in modern drama, some practitioners have de-emphasized the role of the verbal text in favor of the creation of collages, scenarios, rituals or other non-verbal structures which give the actor and his director a greater share of *creative* and less *interpretative* responsibility. But the non-verbal structure is only a different kind of text which still involves some words, and to change the nature of the text is not to destroy

Seeming, Being and Becoming

the actor's involvement with language nor the importance of words as an element of his created mask. Despite the anti-verbal attitude of some contemporary theatre, then, expressive language is an ancient material of great drama, and the literary roots of acting are as strong and as nourishing as any of its other roots. The oldest literary connection for the western actor is found in the *rhapsodes* of classical Greece. These men were considered to be somewhat holy; through a trancelike inspiration from the poet Homer (who was himself regarded as semi-divine), the rhapsodes recited his voluminous works in the marketplace or wherever an audience was to be found. By the way in which divine inspiration worked through them, Plato considered the rhapsodes one of the links in his concept of *the chain of being*.

Ultimate reality for Plato was a realm of pure ideas containing the essence of all forms of the knowable world. These essences could not be known directly but only through various "reflections" which formed the world of sensation. There were, therefore, levels of perception which were closer or farther from ultimate reality, with ordinary sensory perception being several steps removed—a mere reflection of a reflection of a reflection. The gods were close to ultimate reality and holy persons such as oracles, or a great poet like Homer, were man's link to the gods. The rhapsodes were the direct link between ordinary men and the divine poets; the language of their poetry was thus a means whereby a sense of ultimate reality could be passed on to man. Far from being an obstacle to real experience, therefore, great language can be seen as one pathway toward ultimate reality.

Language also serves as a symbolic system which permits man to transmit his wisdom and feelings from one time and place to another; in the science of semantics this function of language is called the "time-binding effect." Before printing and electronic recording techniques, the spoken word was the chief means of time-binding and, so, much of our cultural development was made possible by an *oral tradition*. There have been many types of performers, from rhapsodes to present day folk singers, who have been the instruments of this oral tradition—such performers are generically called *minstrels*.

Historically, the stage actor and the minstrel were closely related through cruel necessity. After the fall of the Roman Empire, the Church (both Eastern and Western) declared theatre a vulgar and outlawed profession. The actor was literally expelled

28

from the theatre, and throughout the Dark and Middle Ages the displaced stage actors took refuge with their brethren minstrels, performing at banquets or other occasions where they could find an audience.

Even outside the theatre, the disfavor of the Church followed the actor; the Council of Laodicea (343-381 A.D.) required all clergy present at a festivity to leave the room before actors were allowed to enter. This ecclesiastical antipathy toward actors lasted for over *seventeen hundred years*; even as late as the fourteenth century Thomas à Becket, who had been friendly toward minstrels while he was Chancellor of the Realm, banned them from his palace once he became Archbishop of Canterbury. Moliere was denied Christian burial in the seventeenth century, and the Church ban against actors in France was not lifted until the Revolution.

Early in this period, a number of Teutonic tribes had migrated into France and England; these Germanic tribes brought with them an oral tradition of their own. They had a special reverence for their minstrels, who were called *scops*. These scops were permanent and respected members of each lord's group of followers, serving as "living newspapers" by celebrating the feats of the lord in their recited sagas; like the Greek rhapsodes, they also served a quasi-religious function as a link between the tribe and its gods. In fact, the most powerful Teutonic god, Odin, was thought to be a performer.

The oral tradition of the Teutons and that of the Latins can be traced through their respective histories until they fuse in the blending of Latin and Germanic cultures during the Middle Ages. Also representative of this tradition were the English *gleeman*, the French *jongleur* and the many itinerant performers called *histriones* who traveled about finding their audiences in castles, inns or by the roadside. These performers combined the sung and spoken word with mime, juggling, acrobatics, dance and instrumental abilities to produce a rich and varied performance tradition. As these wandering minstrels traveled, they carried vernacular languages from one region to another, until eventually they helped to create unified national languages in France and England.

All this went on while stage acting persisted in only a limited way in the miracle, morality and pageant plays sponsored by churches, labor guilds and towns. These were large-scale enterprises often using elaborate effects and pieces of machinery; some of the town pageants lasted as long as forty days, utilizing entire populations and broad areas of the countryside. While there were some theatre "professionals" who were hired to manage and sometimes perform in these elaborate affairs, most of the actors were townspeople. The religious pageants sponsored by labor guilds were likewise performed by the members themselves, so that although theatre in various forms continued in the Middle Ages, it existed mainly as an instrument of religious dogma performed by *amateur* rather than professional actors.

During these centuries, the few professional performers who continued to ply their craft were regarded as little better than pimps or prostitutes, with whom they were often associated and whose functions they often served. Finally in the fifteenth century, the professional actor began to regain his rightful place in his theatre, taking with him the indelible mark of his long association with minstrelsy.

Since words are evocative, the oral performer had no need of elaborate stagecraft. His language and his performance skills were highly portable, so that the oral tradition was also an itinerant tradition. As our own theatre, with the growth of touring and outdoor drama, becomes more and more itinerant in nature, we are re-examining minstrelsy in all its forms as a source of inspiration.

Our ties to the itinerant popular performer reach back through circus, burlesque and vaudeville to the Medicine Show, the Toby Show, and beyond. We have no need to be overawed by the Oriental tradition when we have a performance tradition of our own which encompasses as great a variety of skills. A number of training programs and new theatre groups have begun actively to explore and employ the itinerant oral tradition and we have already begun to experience the way in which this performance form can bind us in a deeply human way to our own cultural roots.

The Tap Root: Mask-wearing

We see that the mask in all its forms—physical, behavioral and verbal—emerges as the central concern of our examination of the genesis of the actor. There is something mysterious and profound in the ability to assume a mask and something timeless and beautiful in the experience of doing so. There is also a sense of abandonment, of license, connected with the wearing of masks; it begins early in our history in primitive ritual, and extends through the Bacchic orgy, the Roman Saturnalia, the medieval Feast of Fools, the great carnivals of the Renaissance and the masked balls of later eras. In all these examples, the same libertinage and ecstasy which marked the worship of Dionysus is carried through time by the wearing of masks. As Jamie Shalleck puts it in his study of masks:

> Certain primitive African tribes believe that a man in a mask is possessed by spirits and thus no longer constrained to act according to human law. In time, the Europeans discovered that masks allowed civilized men and women a degree of freedom that they could not experience otherwise. Soon they were wearing masks to engage in illicit or immoral activities. Prostitutes wore masks. Political intriguers arranged for masked meetings at odd hours of the night. Lovers met in mask at the opera. . . . Halloween

> and masquerade balls [continue today to be] ritual
> celebrations of the mask as a device permitting
> respite from social and moral law.[8]

This mischievous impulse to disguise oneself and, in the safety of the disguise, to behave and experience life in unorthodox ways, seems almost intuitive to man for we see it in the behavior of very young children. Even in the comparative rigidity of maturity, the mimetic impulse remains strong and we continue throughout our lives to delight in the mysterious and often subtle and complex systems of masks which we use in our daily lives. Social psychology in the last decade has been busy exploring the dramaturgy of everyday life; and the processes and the material of the actor are clearly extensions of that daily life. When we realize that the basic processes of acting are distilled and heightened from the mechanisms of everyday social phenomena, however, we must also realize that the actor has a special responsibility to use these common materials to produce uncommon insights. As August Strindberg said to his actors a century ago:

> Acting seems to be the easiest of all the arts
> because everybody walks, talks, stands, gestures
> and makes faces. But then he is just being himself
> and one sees immediately how different that is
> from acting as soon as one puts him on stage and
> gives him a part to learn and interpret.[9]

For the actor, then, the ways in which acting is *different* from everyday life become in the end more important than the ways in which life and acting are similar. Both deserve to be studied and understood, of course, but we sometimes place undue emphasis on the sociology of acting and too little emphasis on its aesthetic possibilities. The actor's ability to transform life into revealing *new* shapes is what enables him to help us see life itself more clearly and deeply.

It is this capacity for *transformation through the wearing of masks* which makes acting such an important art in our age of mass-produced personality, when our culture encourages the development of rigidly conventional responses to life. Theatre is increasingly being

---

[8] *Masks* (New York: Viking Press, 1973), p. 10.
[9] "Notes to the Members of the Intimate Theatre," *Tulane Drama Review* 6, no. 2 (November 1961): p. 156.

seen as possible therapy for such "deadening habit." Most avant-garde theatre is devoted to helping us break down rigid or hypocritical behavioral patterns and to giving us a renewed sense of our own spiritual resources and potentialities.

This is not accomplished without risk. Dionysus is a demanding god; he insists on total commitment from his followers, and at times he can be ruthless and excessive. Such is his nature, because such is that aspect of man's soul which he embodies; he is the irrational, ecstatic, sensual god, and though his potential for joy is very great (it was he who gave us wine), great also is his capacity for disruption. His theatre shares these qualities.

Theatre deals with extremes of human experience and with powerful emotions springing from the very depths of man's existence. Such forces threaten always to overpower their summoners; thus a potential for danger lurks just below the surface of great theatre. It was because of this potential disruptiveness that Plato, for example, regretfully banned the theatre from his ideal Republic. Aristotle answered Plato's fears by showing that the theatre's effect, for all its danger, was usually beneficial; through its cathartic potential, Aristotle argued, theatre helps man to cope with dangerous emotions by arousing and *releasing* them in a controlled, "safe" way.

We can therefore view the actor as our emissary or guide on a journey into potentially dangerous areas of our own existence; via the theatre, we journey into the inferno of our soul and are tempered by the experience. Theatre is our pact with the devil and the actor is our negotiator; transformation through mask-wearing is the central mechanism of this process.

The wearing of masks is also a way for man to objectify his own existence, to come to grips with his own mortality. The deepest, most ancient root of the actor is his *exemplification of man's need and ability to define his own existence.* Moreover, the actor does this with a skill which is itself a kind of potency, a kind of power over the future. While the play itself and the various masks which the actors wear in the play may teach us something about who we are, *the actor's ability to be transformed by wearing his mask teaches us something about whom we may become, reminds us of our ability to redefine our own existence, and his theatre thereby becomes a celebration of the ongoing flow of life.* Ecstasy, we find, means *ek-stasis, to be outside of ourselves.*

Sensing the capacity of the theatre to help enrich our spiritual lives at a time when we have great need for such spiritual revivification, we have begun to explore more than ever before the full richness of the experience which may pass between actor and spectator, and the way in which the theatrical moment can resonate in the totality of our being. The western actor's horizons are thus being continually broadened, and the art of acting has begun to encompass not only an expanding range of performance techniques and possibilities, but a renewed sense of ethical and spiritual purpose as well.

It is a wonderful time to be an actor.

Part Two
Stems and Branches

Stems and branches form the architecture of a plant
Determine its shape
Give it strength and resilience
And are all that we can see of it in the winter.

So well does the actor exemplify man's effort to relate to his own condition that the actor in his theatre has always stood as an exemplar of man in his universe. The acting process has always revealed much of how man has felt, at various times in his history, about the workings of his own mind and about his relationship with his world.

For the Greeks, we have seen, the actor stood as a link in the chain of being; the pantheon of Greek gods and the dramatic myths were the primary components of a great anthropomorphic drama which man projected upon the cosmos. The place of the enactment of these myths, the stage, was the human arena in which destiny was unfolded; so, the ancient actor was an *instrument of destiny*.

In the Roman Empire, man began to worship himself more than his gods; the actor and his theatre were put at the service of a great feast of fashionable sensuality in which the palpability of existence was celebrated. This vulgarization of the ancient religious theatre, its fall from a holy celebration to a mere source of secular pleasure, radically altered the art of acting from that time on.

In marked contrast to the lavishness of the Empire, the centuries which followed were an austere, if not actually dangerous, time for the actor. This was not surprising: Dionysus has had a long reign in a variety of roles and the Middle Ages knew him as Pan or the Devil. It was natural, then, that his theatre, the devil's playground, be banned and that his servant, the actor, be outlawed.

Eventually, however, the Church's antagonism and influence lessened, permitting the return of the actor to the Elizabethan playhouse. With its "Heaven" above and the common man below, Elizabethan theatre stood as a demonstration in miniature of the Elizabethan cosmology; man stood quite literally at the center of the universe, following a destiny mapped out in the stars above. "All the world's a stage," and at the center of the stage-world stood the Elizabethan actor in the afternoon sun, unaided by any but the simplest devices, creating his own world with only his human skills.

After a brief period of renewed religious antagonism and persecution under the government of Oliver Cromwell, which again outlawed the theatre, the spirit of Dionysus was restored to the throne of England in the person of Merry King Charlie. Unfortunately, Dionysus in England turned out to be cheap and perverted; he lost his magnificence and became merely libidinous. His theatre likewise became a libidinous place, favored by whores and whoremasters in the audience, on the stage, and in the plays of the Restoration, many of which feature the "sex chase" as the foundation of their plots. This was a time of tough professionalism for the actor, the time when "show business" as such was invented. The commercial theatre has not changed much since; it remains lusty, bold, gregarious and sensual, but short on spirituality and ethics.

In the eighteenth century, decent folk regained the thrones of England and France and their drama entered a period of sappy sentimentality and stiff neoclassicism. Philosophers of the Age of Reason shifted their attention from the cosmos toward earth, and man became convinced that "the only proper study of mankind is man." This attitude brought with it a new understanding of the importance and dignity of the "ordinary" man; it made possible a radical shift in dramatic subject matter, away from the "larger-than-life" character exemplified by the hero-kings of earlier plays and toward a serious consideration of the people and events of everyday life.

This interest in the mundane world was brought about by humanism, and it set the stage for the development of modern drama. With this new respect for the individual experience, art in all its forms turned toward more subjective and realistic modes during the nineteenth century, the principle movements being *romanticism* and *naturalism*.

Romantic art exalted the subjective experience; the artist's own feelings became important and overt materials in the created work. This inherent romantic subjectivity placed a premium on the personal magnetism of the artist; in all media there emerged towering figures whose personal idiosyncracies and excesses often became the foundations of their artistic styles. In the theatre, actors like Edmund Kean and Sarah Bernhardt became world famous for their highly personal interpretations of great roles. The popular audience loved the bravura of these performers; a role often became a mere vehicle for the actor's display of personal technique.

It was in reaction to the dominance of the virtuoso of the romantic theatre that many late nineteenth- and early twentieth-century theatre artists, like the Duke of Saxe-Meinengen, August Strindberg and Stanislavski himself, began to develop acting companies premised entirely upon ensemble objectives and truthfulness of characterization and opposed to overt theatricality. These efforts usually took a "naturalistic" form.

Naturalism, the other great nineteenth-century movement, arose in the drama in the 1870's and shared its roots with the rise of the empirical method and the "scientific" attitude. Man had begun to think scientifically, or analytically, about everything; it was the popular passion to search out the underlying patterns and causes which motivated everyday events and behavior. In the drama this search resulted in a form dedicated to an almost clinical dissection of the underlying motives of everyday life. Understandably, naturalism eschewed the subjectivity of romanticism in favor of an accurate replication of the minutiae of real life. If romanticism was the *subjective* manifestation of humanist man's obsession with himself, naturalism was its *objective* expression exemplified by the nearly documentary "slice of life" philosophy of Émile Zola and others.

This concern for the accurate representation of reality made the naturalistic theatre one consumed with a passion for illusion. The pursuit of verisimilitude challenged both the ingenuity of the scenic designer and the emotional technique of the actor. Thus, the nineteenth- and early twentieth-century theatre became very much a theatre of illusion, of *seeming*.

Besides this passion for realistic illusion, empiricism also brought to nineteenth- and early twentieth-century acting a passion for *principle* and *system*. For the first time, actors and directors began to seek formulas and to construct systems which, if followed, would produce the desired kind of performance. These systems took two principal forms: some, like the system of François Delsarte (1811-1871), were highly mechanical in nature, suggesting ways of establishing the actor's gesture or posture based upon psychophysical principles; others were systems concerned more with the actor's internal condition than with his external form.

These two branches of thought, one essentially objective and the other subjective, are the pivotal attitudes in the development of acting in our century. Both, despite their obvious differences, reflect nineteenth- and early twentieth-century man's preoccupation with the workings of his own mind.

The First Branch: Stanislavski

Constantin Stanislavski (1863-1938) is the most important single figure in the history of acting. He gave us an expression of fundamental objectives, a sense of seriousness and a focus on the spirituality of the actor which have been major influences on most contemporary theatre, both naturalistic and non-naturalistic. Although he is most often associated with naturalism, his practice was not limited to the original objectives of nineteenth-century naturalism.

The nineteenth-century naturalists had seen the inevitable effect of heredity and environment as the "scientific" truth underlying human behavior. They believed that this truth could be communicated on the stage if, as Émile Zola put it, "one simply takes from life the history of a being, or of a group of beings, whose acts one faithfully records."[1] The naturalistic actor was therefore expected to submerse himself entirely in the life of his character so that it became "his own." Zola anticipated Stanislavski when he said that the actors should "not *play*; but rather *live* before the audience."[2] It was this new sense of acting as a way of attaining states of independent, self-sufficient reality that later formed the central motivation of Stanislavski's work.

While he shared this central impulse of the naturalists, however, Stanislavski wished to go far beyond the clinically accurate and

[1] Quoted by Oscar Brockett in *The Theatre: An Introduction* (New York: Holt, Rinehart, and Winston, 1964), pp. 275-76.
[2] *Ibid.*

41

objective representation suggested by Zola; he wished the actor not only to represent reality, but also to create a *subjective* reality of his own: "Those who think that we sought naturalism on the stage," he said, "are mistaken. We never leaned toward such a principle.... We sought inner truth, the truth of feeling and experience."[3]

Jerzy Grotowski, director of the Polish Laboratory Theatre, calls Stanislavski's technique *existential naturalism*. This phrase captures perfectly Stanislavski's wish to go beyond simple representation and to create on the stage a new, *independent* reality. The main objective of Stanislavski's work was to lead the actor to *metamorphosis*, meaning literally *meta-morphose*, a *form above* or a transcendent reality. Speaking of merely representational acting, Stanislavski said that "the difference between my art and that is the difference between 'seeming' and 'being'."[4]

In his search for *being*, Stanislavski developed ways of heightening the personal involvement of the actor in his own performance. The most famous aspect of his training was his "psychotechnique," a set of exercises and principles designed to help the actor involve his own personal feelings and experiences in the creation of his role. Through self-discipline, life observation and the development of total concentration, Stanislavski's actor learned to "recall" particular emotional sensations from his own life which were analogous to those experienced by the character. Armed with his disciplined memory for sensation and emotion, the actor then opened himself to experience what the character experienced *as if* it were actually happening to him. By thus putting himself totally in the place of the character, the actor was able to construct a performance which became a *real* experience for him, not merely the re-enactment or representation of a fiction. Although Stanislavski's actor always worked from the basis of his own personal self ("always be yourself on stage," he taught), the actor's self was metamorphosed into a new self by the power of the experiences of the character, the experiences were happening *as if* to the actor himself. Just as we are formed by the experiences and conditions of our lives, so Stanislavski's actor allowed himself to be re-formed by the experiences of his character-as-if-himself, permitting him to truly *be* in the reality of his character.

[3] Elizabeth Reynolds Hapgood, ed. and trans., *Stanislavski: An Actor's Handbook* (New York: Theatre Arts Books, 1963), p. 100.
[4] *Ibid.*, p. 91.

One of the greatest obstacles to the actor in his striving to *be* on the stage, Stanislavski believed, was an excessive awareness of his audience. This audience awareness encouraged *self*-consciousness in the actor, making impossible a total involvement in the character's reality. Stanislavski's antidote for this destructive kind of performance awareness was the related skills of relaxation and concentration; he wanted his actor to be as concentrated and relaxed in public as he could be in private. Stanislavski himself had discovered this state of liberated concentration during an early exercise: his teacher had given him the simple task of counting the nails in the stage floor and, in his total concentration on his task, Stanislavski found that he totally lost his self-consciousness and achieved a heightened involvement in his own stage reality. Much of the psycho-technique he later developed was aimed at developing the actor's ability to focus concentration in such a total and free-flowing way.

We can better understand this principle of relaxed concentration if we examine an early lesson with a group of students taught by Stanislavski's colleague Eugene Vakhtangov. One of the students has been asked to go to one corner of the studio to prepare a brief exercise while Vakhtangov continues a class discussion. Gradually Vakhtangov turns the attention of the class to the student, who by this time is busy rehearsing his scene and is unaware that his rehearsal has become a performance observed by the class.

There is much laughter as the student finally realizes that he has been watched. During the discussion following the incident, the student reports that he has experienced a sense of liberation through his unself-conscious involvement in his "accidental" performance. Vakhtangov then counsels him:

> Remember these moments. They were moments
> of "public solitude." They came to you naturally,
> organically, when some concrete action or
> thought compelled you to forget the audience.
> Usually, an actor playing this "public solitude"
> scene tries to persuade himself: "I'm alone, alone,
> alone. There's no audience. I don't hear the
> spectators, I don't feel them: I'm alone!" It is a kind
> of self-persuasion, but a bad one. Why persuade
> yourself that there are no spectators when they're
> there, two or three yards away, living, watching,
> breathing, coughing, laughing! After all, you're

> acting for *them*, not for yourself. This forceable
> alienation from the audience is senseless, it
> contradicts the very essence of acting.
> Stanislavski says so too.[5]

From this statement we can see that Stanislavski in no way wished the actor to deny the public conditions under which he worked, but rather to accept and utilize these theatrical conditions so completely that they became assimilated into the reality of the performance. As Stanislavski himself put it, "there is no such thing as actuality on the stage. Art is the product of the imagination as the work of the dramatist should be. The aim of the actor should be to turn the play into a theatrical reality."[6]

Unfortunately, Stanislavski's sense of a *theatrical* reality has occasionally been lost by those who have brought his system to other countries. Some of his disciples have put such stress on the actor's privacy that they have sometimes lost Stanislavski's sense of the public theatrical situation, producing an uncraftsmanlike and indulgently subjective actor whom Stanislavski certainly would not have admired. At the same time, there have been many who carried on Stanislavski's work in valid ways, and most of the acting teachers of major significance in America are among them.

There were others, of course, who had fundamental disagreements with Stanislavski's principles even while his work was developing. Some of his contemporaries argued that the Stanislavskian "solitude," however public or craftsmanlike it could be, required the actor to deny the overtly communal nature of the theatre. This point of view has been shared by many since who have felt that Stanislavski's form was "anti-theatrical," locking the audience into the passive role of observer and ruling out its participation as a *co-creator*. Even the man Stanislavski thought taught his system better than anyone else, Vakhtangov, came to feel this way later in life:

> Stanislavski demanded . . . that the audience
> forget that it is in the theatre, that it came to feel
> itself living in the atmosphere and milieu in
> which the characters of the play live. He rejoiced
> in the fact that the audience used to come to
> the Moscow Art Theatre to *The Three Sisters*, not as
> to a theatre, but as if invited to the Prosorov

[5] From a privately circulated translation.
[6] *Stanislavski: An Actor's Handbook*, pp. 159-60.

house. This he considered to be the highest
achievement of the theatre. Stanislavski wanted
to destroy theatrical banality, he wanted to put
and end to it at once. Whatever reminded him
of the old theatres even to the slightest extent,
he branded with the word "theatrical," this word
having become a term of abuse in the Moscow
Art Theatre. To be sure, what he was
berating was vulgar indeed, but carried away by
the need for ferreting out vulgarity, Stanislavski
also removed a certain genuine, necessary
theatricality, and genuine theatricality consists
in presenting theatrical works in a theatrical
manner.[7]

Stanislavski's emphasis on realistic means at the possible expense
of theatricality was understandable, however; he was reacting
against a mannered and artificialized nineteenth-century theatre,
a style of bravura performance which he termed "rubber stamp"
acting.

Furthermore, he was responding positively to the new and
important urge in man to examine the workings of his own mind,
and like the work of all artists of his period, his work shows the
enormous influence of the rise of the science of psychology. This
fledgling discipline, itself deeply rooted in the arts and particularly
in the drama, was at this time beginning its systematic inquiry into
the operation of the mind. The theatre began to adopt much of the
attitude and vocabulary of this new science; the importance of past
experiences and of memory in Freudian psychology, for example,
was matched by the importance of sensory and emotional memory
in Stanislavski's acting technique. The unconscious as a source of
motivation and emotional power was systematically explored by
actors and analysts alike: acting began to dissect the behavior of
everyday life until character study became more important than
dramatic action. Where the classical actor had revealed destiny, the
naturalistic actor began to reveal only motivation.[8]

Freud and Stanislavski both assumed that human behavior was
motivated as much by suppressed memories as by the immediate
situation; both focused attention on a motivational process by

---

[7] "Fantastic Realism," in *Directors on Directing*, Toby Cole and Helen Chinoy, ed. (Indianapolis:
Bobbs-Merrill, 1953), p. 185.
[8] A persistent naturalist would, perhaps, argue that human motivation is in fact the mechanism
or even the source of "destiny."

which they believed that human action sprang out of the memory filled unconscious into the conscious present. Our present-day view of the mind, on the other hand, is that of a single, tot. organismic field comprised of past and present, conscious an unconscious, physical and spiritual aspects, all inseparably inte: mingled. The unconscious as an identifiably separate area of th personality is less important to us today and so, therefore, an memory and motivation less important in our drama and in ou contemporary actor training.

Instead, our theatre, influenced by our psychology just a Stanislavski was influenced by his, stresses the immediate interac tion of self and environment. As in current psychological practice our theatre tends to utilize intimate, direct and immediate experi ence expressed through a wide spectrum of sensation. Is it an wonder, then, that from our point of view the particularly Freud ian and realistic form of performance practiced by Stanislavski ha passed into the pantheon of great theatrical styles, respected and often revived, but no longer operating as an immediate force in today's theatrical culture?

Nevertheless, Stanislavski's vision, his central impulse if not hi: form, is still very much alive in our theatre, not only in our traditional theatre but also in the work of the avant-garde such as Jerzy Grotowski, Julian Beck, Joseph Chaikin, Richard Schechner and others of equally disparate persuasions. This central vision was of the performance not as a *reflection* of reality, but as a reality *unto itself*. It is this impulse away from *seeming* and toward *being* that we must gratefully credit to Stanislavski. If we liberate Stanislavski's principles from the inevitably Freudian and realistic vocabulary in which they were expressed, we find that he remains the great fountainhead of inspiration for a variety of today's theatre, and that his objectives are still very much our own.

The Second Branch: Meyerhold

The main objection to Stanislavski's naturalism was that it denied the overtly communal and participatory nature of theatre. This idea was of central importance to the work of Vsevelod Meyerhold (1874-1942). In 1905, Stanislavski appointed him to lead an experimental group seeking new methods. Despite this generous gesture by Stanislavski, Meyerhold soon separated from the Moscow Art Theatre because of his objections to what he called Stanislavski's "Theatre of Mood."

Meyerhold felt that Stanislavski attempted to create so complete and self-contained a world on the stage that there was nothing left for the audience to contribute. Meyerhold was encouraged in this point of view by an idea borrowed from the philosopher Schopenhauer, which he quoted thus:

> A work of art can function only through the imagination. Therefore a work of art must constantly arouse the imagination, not just arouse, but activate. . . . [To arouse the imagination] is a necessary condition of an esthetic phenomenon, and also a basic law of the fine arts. It therefore follows that an artistic work must *not* supply everything to our senses but only enough to direct our imagination onto the right path, leaving the last word to our imagination.[9]

9"The Theatre Theatrical" in *Directors on Directing*, pp. 165-66.

Seeming, Being and Becoming

Meyerhold was outraged by the way in which Stanislavski's theatre, to his mind, forced the spectator into the passive role of a "voyeur." Instead, he wished to accept the audience as an equal and active partner in the act of creation; he proposed to do this by creating a performance which presented stimulation to the audience's imagination, rather than one which represented reality for the audience merely to observe.

For Stanislavski, the essential life of the performance was located on the stage and within the actor's experience; but for Meyerhold it was located in that point of encounter between stage and audience where the forcefulness of the stage image entered the consciousness of the spectator and resonated in his imagination. The naturalistic theatre had, Meyerhold felt, de-emphasized the encounter between actor and spectator and had become instead a director's theatre in which the work of the author and the actor were shaped by the director's production concept. He called this a "triangular theatre" (see fig. 1A).

Meyerhold's own theatre was designed not as a triangle, but as a "straight line" (see fig. 1B) in which the confrontation of actor and spectator was central: "After incorporating the author's work by way of the director," he said, "the actor comes face to face with the spectator (author and director at the actor's back), and acts *freely* while enjoying the give and take between the two main elements of a theatre—the player and the playgoer."[10]

[10] *Ibid.*, p. 172.

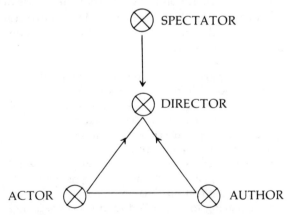

Figure 1A: The Triangular Theatre. Meyerhold probably means that the spectator witnesses the production entirely through the director's concept and control, rather than through the director as a person.

48

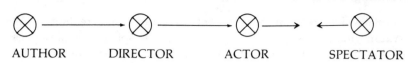

AUTHOR   DIRECTOR   ACTOR   SPECTATOR

Figure 1B: The Straight Line Theatre. Although he allowed for a "free" interaction of actor and spectator, Meyerhold's sculpturally precise form would not have allowed much variance from the rehearsed performance; the difference was one of *attitude* and the kind of planning which went into the performance.

To heighten this sense of give and take between stage and audience, Meyerhold encouraged the actor to "never forget that he is performing before an audience, with a stage beneath his feet and a set around him."[11] In this Meyerhold is diametrically opposed to the Stanislavskian idea of "public solitude." By allowing the fact of the performance to remain obvious, Meyerhold meant to remind the audience that it was witnessing a work of the imagination to which it could contribute: "Ultimately, the stylistic method presupposes the existence of a fourth *creator* in addition to the author, the director and the actor—namely, the spectator."[12] This active creative participation by the audience is a hallmark of much contemporary theatre and is one of the most important of Meyerhold's influences.

In order to keep the stage image suggestive or *presentational* rather than representational, Meyerhold designed it to be somewhat abstract or "incomplete," a careful selection of certain essential qualities of real life presented in a stylized form. As he put it, "the stylized theatre produces a play in such a way that the spectator is compelled to employ his imagination *creatively* in order to *fill in* those details *suggested* by the stage action."[13] Meyerhold was suggesting here not less emphasis on the truth of the performance nor simply a truth represented on the stage which the audience observed, but rather a performance which presented the truth in a form accessible to the spectator's creatively imaginative participation. While Stanislavski's actor recreated a heightened sense of real life, Meyerhold's actor gestured boldly in highly compositional, nearly "dancelike" ways.

Like Stanislavski's principles, Meyerhold's ideas have sometimes been misapplied by followers who have achieved merely sculptural effects at the expense of deeper truth. Meyerhold's stylization, like

[11] Edward Braun, ed. and trans., *Meyerhold on Theatre* (New York: Hill & Wang, 1969), p. 63.
[12] *Ibid.*
[13] *Ibid.*

49

Seeming, Being and Becoming

Stanislavski's realism, was meant to serve inner feelings: "As Wagner makes his orchestra speak about the spiritual experiences of his heroes," Meyerhold said, "so I make plastic movements express inner feelings."[14]

Meyerhold's stylized theatre was premised on plastic (sculptural) principles, which he felt allowed for greater suggestiveness than strictly lifelike behavior. He even likened theatrical response to that evoked by a painting:

> When one looks at a painting, one is always aware that it is composed of paint, canvas, and brush strokes, but none the less it creates a heightened and clarified impression of life. Frequently, the more obvious the artifice, the more powerful the impression of life.[15]

Meyerhold felt that naturalism's concern for lifelikeness had overwhelmed its concern for aesthetic excellence, so that naturalistic acting carried the imperfections of everyday life onto the stage without refinement, while his own stylized theatre allowed the actor to present an idealized or purified image of life as it "ought to be":

> The actor in the Naturalistic Theatre is extremely nimble at transforming himself, but his methods do not originate from *plastic* action but from make-up and an onomatopoeic imitation of various accents, dialects and voices. Instead of developing his esthetic sense to exclude all coarseness, the actor's task [in naturalism] is to lose his self-consciousness. A photographic sense of recording daily trivia is instilled in [him].[16]

Instead of mimicking real life, Meyerhold's stylistic actor worked according to a set of pristine physical principles which transformed the appearance of everyday life and artistically purified it: "The New Theatre changed the absurd ornateness of the naturalistic theatres," Meyerhold said, "into a structural plan based on rhythmic, linear movement and musical harmony of colours."[17]

---

[14] *Directors on Directing*, p. 176.
[15] *Meyerhold on Theatre*, p. 63.
[16] *Directors on Directing*, p. 165.
[17] *Ibid.*, p. 177.

To teach his actors this sense of plasticity, Meyerhold developed a special training program called *biomechanics*. As its name suggests, it derived compositional and rhythmic principles from the biological structure of the body. It was deeply influenced by the old discipline of eurhythmics and also by the Oriental theatre; biomechanics literally meant "the power of pantomine." Where Stanislavski's training emphasized psychological discipline, Meyerhold emphasized physical technique.

To give each its due, the acting techniques of Stanislavski and Meyerhold are two paths toward different but equally valid theatrical truths. The disagreements between them are finally matters of individual taste and persist today between those who work from the "inside out" and those who work from the "outside in." Serious actors of either school, however, continue to be concerned with the truthfulness and artistic integrity of their result.

The Branches Intertwine: Vakhtangov, Brecht

Eugene Vakhtangov (1883-1922) worked with Stanislavski and Meyerhold and admired them both. Although he won Stanislavski's admiration as the best teacher of the Stanislavski system, Vakhtangov remained aware of the shortcomings of naturalism. He attempted a compromise between the Stanislavski and Meyerhold systems in his own approach to acting, which he called "Fantastic Realism." This was fundamentally a realistic form, but one in which the selected details of performance were abstracted and exaggerated in order to stimulate the audience's imagination. Vakhtangov was, in a sense, attempting to use Stanislavski's means for Meyerhold's ends.

Radical German playwright and director Bertolt Brecht (1898-1956) was much influenced by Vakhtangov and he described the relationship of Stanislavski, Meyerhold and Vakhtangov in this way:

> *Progressiveness of Stanislavski's method.* 1. The fact that it's a method. 2. Closer knowledge of man, the private element. 3. Psychological contradictions can be portrayed (end of the moral categories of good and evil). 4. Allowance for influence of the environment. 5. Latitude. 6. Naturalness of portrayal.

> *Vakhtangov's method.* 1. Theatre is theatre. 2. The how, not the what. 3. More composition. 4. Greater inventiveness and imagination.

Seeming, Being and Becoming

> *Meyerhold's method.* 1. Against the private element.
> 2. Emphasis on virtuosity. 3. Movement and its
> mechanics. 4. Abstraction of the environment.
>
> *The meeting point.* Vakhtangov, who embraces the
> other two as contradictory elements but is at the
> same time the freest. By comparison, Meyerhold
> is strained, Stanislavski slack; the latter an
> imitation of life, the former an abstraction.[18]

Brecht drew his own conclusions and applications from Vakhtangov's method; what he admired most was the way it extended real-life behavior into an almost *sur*-real form without losing a clear association to real life. By abstracting and heightening real-life behavior, Brecht believed, Vakhtangov made it more accessible to the audience's scrutiny and judgment: the performance became not merely a representation of real-life behavior but a *demonstration* which could reveal new truths about that behavior.

Brecht, along with his colleague Erwin Piscator, extended Vakhtangov's principles in order to make the actor's demonstration communicate in a precise and didactic way: "but when Vakhtangov's actor says 'I'm not laughing, I'm demonstrating laughter'," said Brecht, "one still doesn't learn anything from his demonstration."[19] Brecht used the surreal quality of Vakhtangov's acting technique to permit a kind of "editorializing"; while the actor, for example, is singing the lovely melody of "Mack the Knife," we realize that the lyrics are in fact blood-curdling, so that the tension between form and content forces us to a shocking realization of Brecht's point of view. By using the actor's demonstration as a teaching device, Brecht's theatre became *an instrument of social change.* In this way his work set the tone for the spirit of *usefulness* which pervades today's theatre.

Brecht's desire to *change* rather than simply to *reveal* human behavior set his idea of acting apart from all that had gone before, and he searched for an entirely new theatrical form. Aristotle had described the dramatic form as dealing with individual events and lives within the limits of time and place suitable to the magnitude of a theatrical performance; Brecht wished to condense time and space and to treat events on a larger societal scope. He was forced beyond the limits of what Aristotle would have called the purely

---

[18] John Willett, ed. and trans., *Brecht on Theatre* (New York: Hill & Wang, 1957), pp. 237-38.
[19] *Ibid.*

dramatic form and began to use narrative devices similar to those which Aristotle described for the *epic* poem. Thus Brecht called his theatre an *Epic Theatre.*

With its focus on the action of men within a broad societal scope, Brecht's theatre was dedicated to social reform. It was from his humanitarian emotion, inspired primarily by his experiences as an ambulance driver in World War I, that Brecht derived his theatrical objective: society, Brecht believed, could be changed by changing the individuals of whom it was comprised, and the live theatre could be one of the best instruments of this reform.

In order to pursue this use of the theatre, however, Brecht had to make some new assumptions about the nature of the human mind. The naturalists had assumed that personality was determined by heredity and environment, but Brecht was more in tune with the contemporary view that the personality is continually developing and changing:

> We who are concerned to change human as well as
> ordinary nature must find means of "shedding
> light on" the human being at that point where he
> seems capable of being changed by society's
> intervention. This means a quite new attitude on
> the part of the actor, for his art has hitherto been
> based on the assumption that people are what
> they are, and will remain so whatever it may cost
> society or themselves: "indestructably human,"
> "you can't change human nature," and so on. . . .
> So our theatre's significant stage groupings are
> not just an effect or a "purely esthetic" phe-
> nomenon, conducive to formal beauty. They are a
> part of a hugely-conceived theatre for the new
> social order, and they cannot be achieved without
> deep understanding and passionate support of the
> new structure of human relations.[20]

Brecht believed that in order to be understood, human behavior had to be seen in its social perspective or "historical field." Accordingly, Brecht was attracted to old tales and argued against modernizing old plays since their remoteness in time helps us to perceive the *Gest* or *context* of the action, making it easier to criticize and judge within a sociological perspective. The "distanced" perspective of older plays was more difficult to achieve in contempo-

[20] *Ibid.,* p. 235.

rary plays, Brecht reasoned, because of the audience's closeness to the world of the play. Devices had to be found, he felt, to provide substitute sources of distance in the newer plays: "These new sources of distance," he said, "are only designed to free socially-conditioned phenomena from that stamp of familiarity which protects them against our grasp today."[21]

These new sources of distance comprised what Brecht called the *verfremdungseffect*. *Verfremdung* literally means "strange-making" although this term has been widely translated as "alienation," an unfortunate rendering which inaccurately connotes a lack of involvement or emotion. Brecht pointed out that his Epic Theatre

> in no way renounces emotion. Least of all
> emotions like the love of justice, the urge to
> freedom or justified anger: so little does it
> renounce these emotions, that it does not rely on
> their being there, but tries to strengthen or to
> evoke them. The "critical attitude" into which it is
> trying to put its public cannot be passionate
> enough.[22]

What Brecht did renounce was the sort of "easy" sentimentality which was premised on an indiscriminate kind of identification of the spectator with the character. While a great deal of misunderstanding and obfuscation has surrounded Brecht's idea of *verfremdung*, all it really meant was that we ought to care passionately about the *point* of the demonstration without becoming unduly caught up in the demonstration *itself*.

This nearly clinical attitude in the spectator, Brecht believed, had to be established by the actor who adopted his own "critical attitude" toward his character. This sense of purposeful distance between actor and character was a radically different relationship than the identification of actor and character espoused by Stanislavski. Brecht described this new relationship:

> The demonstrator in the theatre, the actor, must
> employ a technique by means of which he can
> render the tone of the person demonstrated with
> a certain reserve, with a certain distance (allowing
> the spectator to say: "now he's getting excited,

---

[21] *Ibid.*, p. 192.
[22] Quoted by Martin Esslin in *Brecht: The Man and His Work* (Garden City, N.Y.: Doubleday 1960), p. 150.

its no use, too late, at last," etc.). In short, the
actor must remain a demonstrator. He
must render the person demonstrated as a different person. He must not leave out of his
presentation the "*he* did this, he said that." He
must not let himself be completely transformed into the person demonstrated.[23]

The actor's purpose in Brecht's theatre, then, was to perform
selected but recognizable details of human behavior in a manner
and context which caused them to seem suddenly unfamiliar and
revealing, permitting the audience to perceive and judge them
more clearly. The performance was prepared as if it were *evidence*
upon which the audience had been asked to pass judgment.

In all, Brecht's contribution to our contemporary theatre lies not
so much in his theorizing (though it has been important) as in his
desire for the passionate and direct involvement of the actor in the
day-to-day life of his society and his insistence on the moral
obligation of the theatre artist to make his world a better place to
live. While many reject Brecht's Epic principles, every major figure
in today's avant-garde theatre would agree with his poem which
summarizes Brecht's sense of the moral responsibilities of the
theatre:

> Actors
> You who perform plays in great houses
> Under false suns and before silent faces
> Look sometimes at
> The theatre who's stage is the street.
>
> Look—the man at the corner re-enacting
> The accident.
>
> If you declare,
> He is no artist,
> He may reply:
> You are not men.
> A worse reproach by far.
> Declare instead:
> He is an artist because a man.
> What he does we may do

---

[23] "The Epic Theatre," in *Directors on Directing*, pp. 239-40.

Seeming, Being and Becoming

With more perfection
Thus gaining honor.

But let us understand each other.
You may perform better than he
Whose stage is the street,
Still your achievement will be less
If your theatre is less
Meaningful than his,
If it touches less
Deeply the lives of those who watch.

If its reasons
Are less,
Or its usefulness.[24]

The Actor as Signmaker: Artaud

Despite their differences, Stanislavski, Meyerhold, Vakhtangov and Brecht had one fundamental thing in common: however each approached the question of "stylizing" stage behavior, they all believed that the actor's performance was meant to evoke a direct association with everyday life. Even the highly plastic forms of Meyerhold were designed to excite a sense of the inner feelings of the characters, and Brecht's demonstrations were aimed at analyzing the behavior of real people in relation to their environment. All of these acting techniques, then, even those with a heightened sense of composition, remained essentially *mimetic* in the original sense of that term; the differences between mimetic and nonmimetic art are of crucial importance in understanding much contemporary theatre.

Mimetic art must have an *object*, something outside of itself to which it refers, the thing, in short, that it is "about." To some degree, the effectiveness of mimetic art is increased by our ability to associate the work of art with its object. Mimetic acting is therefore partly dependent upon our ability to recognize its object, and such a performance suffers when it fails to relate us directly to qualities of experience familiar in everyday life. For example, some critics believed that Meyerhold's sculptural theatre went so far in its stylization that the performance ceased to relate to real life at all and became totally abstract; from this point of view, Meyerhold's actor had verged out of drama and into pure dance. Charging such formalism, the Russian government later abandoned

Seeming, Being and Becoming

Meyerhold's theatre as being too "formalistic" for the common man to understand and ruled that Soviet acting return to a Stanislavskian realism.

Nevertheless, much of today's avant-garde has gone on challenging the assumption that acting must be fundamentally representional or mimetic. Mimetic art, it is argued, is always one step removed from the reality it portrays; if a performance attempts to create the illusion that the actor and the stage are something other than what they really are, then the performance is trapped inescapably in a condition of *seeming* and is incapable of true *being*. The alternative is to attempt to create a nonmimetic or (as it is called in painting) nonobjective theatre which would be based not upon representation in any form, but instead, upon confronting the audience with raw, primary experience *per se*. This impulse is summarized in the statement that "a poem should not *mean*, but *be*," and has been important in writing, painting, music, happenings and other modern art forms; in the theatre its most important manifestation has been in the work of Antonin Artaud (1896-1948) and the later work he influenced.

Artaud proposed a theatre of spiritual experience whose form was not necessarily premised on everyday life at all: "the images of poetry in the theatre," he said, "are a spiritual force that begins its trajectory in the senses and does without reality altogether."[25] This nonmimetic theatrical force expressed itself through the sensory or visceral impact of the performance on the audience:

> Illusion will no longer depend upon the credibility
> or incredibility of the action, but upon the
> communicative power and reality of that
> action. . . . The spectator who comes to our
> theatre knows that he is taking part in a true
> action involving not only his mind but his very
> senses and flesh.[26]

Artaud called his physically overwhelming and nonmimetic theatre a "Theatre of Cruelty."

Artaud's idea of "cruelty" has been often misunderstood. He did not mean physical suffering alone:

[25] *The Theatre and Its Double* (New York: Grove Press, 1958), p. 25.
[26] *Ibid.*, pp. 44-45.

> The word "cruelty" must be taken in a broad sense
> and not in the rapacious physical sense that it is
> customarily given. . . . From the point of view of
> the mind, cruelty signifies rigor, implacable
> intention and decision, irreversible and absolute
> determination. . . . Cruelty is above all lucid, a
> kind of rigid control and submission to
> necessity.[27]

While he did admit the possibility of bodily pain as an element of
the theatrical experience, his real objective was to produce an
experience so complete and acute in its sensory appeal that the
spectator would be overcome: "I propose then a theatre in which
violent images crush and hypnotize the sensibility of the spectator
seized by the theatre as by a whirlwind of higher forces.[28]

The means toward this theatre suggested themselves to Artaud
in 1931 when he witnessed a performance by a Balinese dance
troupe at the Colonial Exhibition in Paris. As he watched the
dancers creating what he called "animated Hieroglyphs," he began
to think of "a new physical language, based upon signs and no
longer upon words."[29] The function of the actor, Artaud decided,
would in no way be the representation of human behavior; the
ideal actor would instead be a *maker of signs*.

The actor's signs were to take the form of profoundly spiritual
gestures, which, when performed "with the force required, incites
the organism and, through it, the entire individuality to take
attitudes in harmony with the gesture.[30] These profound sign-
gestures would be the result, Artaud believed, of a radical actor-
training process called "affective athleticism." Affective athleticism is similar in principle to Meyerhold's biomechanics, as it is
based on the relationship of physical centers, the breath, bodily
functions, emotions, and the soul. Artaud's specific descriptions of
the process are vague and incomplete, involving an adaptation of
Chinese psychophysiology as used by acupuncturists.[31] The actor
devoting himself totally to this system, Artaud believed, could

[27] *Ibid.*, pp. 101-2.
[28] *Ibid.*, pp. 82-83.
[29] *Ibid.*, p. 54.
[30] *Ibid.*, pp. 81-82.
[31] Acupuncture is one of three types of Chinese medicine and is widely practiced today. In acupuncture specific nerves are stimulated or anesthetized by the skillful insertion of needles into the body: hence the name, *acupuncture*. The technique is now being used as an anesthetic process in the West.

eventually express, like a man in a trance, the deepest impulses of his soul through his gestures. Then, when the spectator empathically mirrored the actor's gesture within his own organism, the force of that gesture would penetrate the spectator's being very like an acupuncturist's needle and the actor's spiritual condition would be recreated in him.

Artaud's specific model for the actor was a *martyr being burnt alive, still making signs to us through the flames.* The violence of this image was appropriate to the degree of force which Artaud felt was necessary to overcome the habitual defenses of the spectator. His most famous work, *The Theatre and Its Double*, compared the potential force of the theatre to the most cruel natural force which he could think of, the Great Bubonic Plague.

> The theatre like the plague is a crisis which is
> resolved by death or cure. . . . From the human
> point of view, the action of the theatre, like that of
> plague, is beneficial, for impelling men to see
> themselves as they are, it causes the mask to fall,
> reveals the lie, the slackness, baseness, and
> hypocrisy of our world.[32]

Artaud's desire to cause "the mask to fall" from what he saw as a corrupt Western society established a "therapeutic" objective for the theatrical experience. Underlying this therapeutic effort was the assumption that authentic man was pure and had been corrupted by civilization, imprisoned in a veneer of conventional hypocrisy. The theatre, he believed, could force man back to a pure, "natural" state. Artaud was therefore a spiritual anarchist, an advocate (like Dionysus) of irrational and sensory states of being and an enemy of rational convention and logic.

Western theatre, he felt, had abandoned its roots in the irrational and had fallen under the dictatorship of words, psychology and rationality. In Artaud's theatre, he hoped, the actor's signs would instead bypass our conceptual mind altogether and affect us directly through the nervous system and nonrational motor responses. Such a theatre would become a primary experience with no reference beyond itself; it would cease to *seem* altogether and come instead to *be* totally in its own right. Artaud was

---

[32] *The Theatre and Its Double*, pp. 31-32.

proposing a theatre whose true material was a kind of controlled madness and whose objectives were neither psychological nor political, but spiritual. Such a theatre would surely have pleased Dionysus, whose influence, thanks to Artaud, is very much at work today.

The Holy Actor: Grotowski

Despite his official communist atheism, no one in Western theatre has pursued the spirituality of the actor as a maker of signs further than Jerzy Grotowski of the Polish Laboratory Theatre. He describes the actor as *holy*, although he defines holiness in a very specific way:

> One must not take the word "holy" in the
> religious sense. It is rather a metaphor defining a
> person who, through his art, climbs upon the
> stake and performs an act of self-sacrifice.[33]

As did Artaud, Grotowski believes that man's "unspoiled" condition is inherently good. In man's "authentic" state he is a totally integrated being whose physical and spiritual aspects are harmoniously intertwined; it is the encrustations of social living, Grotowski believes, which obstruct the immediate expression of our deepest and purest impulses.

The actor's first task, therefore, is the removal of these obstructions. He must use his acting discipline and the performance itself as the occasion for a profound act of self-penetration and revelation which will return him to a pure spiritual state. Through such an act of "uncovering" the actor undergoes the same sort of beatification through selflessness as does a saint in his martyrdom. Grotowski applies this religious metaphor very literally in his

---

[33] *Towards a Poor Theatre* (New York: Simon & Schuster, 1968), p. 43.

productions, most of which revolve around the magic enactment of a myth of sacrifice by an actor-priest. *The Constant Prince* enacted a crucifixion within the walls of a small arena (likened by Grotowski to an operating theatre) into which a small number of witnesses peered from above; *Faustus* was a banquet at which the Faust figures were literally eaten; *Akropolis* was a ritual enactment of the concentration camp cremations.

Appropriate to the idea of the actor's sacrificial uncovering, Grotowski calls his training system an "eradication of blocks," a *Via Negativa*, a progressive elimination of the obstacles between the actor's pure impulse and its observable manifestation. As he describes it:

> The education of an actor in our theatre is not
> a matter of teaching him something; we attempt
> to eliminate his organism's resistance to the
> psychic process. The result is freedom from the
> time-lapse between inner impulse and outer re-
> action in such a way that the impulse is already
> an outer reaction. Impulse and action are
> concurrent: the body vanishes, burns, and the
> spectator sees only a series of visible impulses.[34]

Grotowski refers to Artaud specifically as a source of this theatrical thinking, and these "visible impulses" are the spiritual gestures or signs of which Artaud had spoken.

Grotowski's signs would have pleased not only Artaud but Meyerhold as well, since they are based not on everyday life but rather are aesthetically composed out of the actor's studies, heightened and arranged by Grotowski and his dramaturg. Grotowski believes, as did Meyerhold, that heightened composition actually facilitates communication:

> We find that artificial composition not only does
> not limit the spiritual but actually leads to it. . . .
> The forms of common "natural" behavior obscure
> the truth; we compose a role as a system of signs
> which demonstrate what is behind the mask of
> common vision: the dialectics of human
> behavior. . . . A man in an elevated spiritual state
> uses rhythmically articulated signs, begins to

[34] *Ibid.*, p. 16.

dance, to sing. A *sign*, not a common gesture, is the
elementary integer of expression for us.[35]

Artaud had seen the Eastern theatre, with its highly developed
and fixed vocabulary of signs, as the model for the reform of
Western acting. Although Grotowski has studied at a classical
Chinese theatre and uses many Oriental ideas and training devices, he rejects the Oriental idea of a traditional vocabulary of
signs:

In terms of formal technique, we do not work
by proliferation of signs, or by accumulation of
signs (as in the formal repetitions of Oriental
theatre). Rather, we subtract, seeking *distillation*
of signs by eliminating those elements of
"natural" behavior which obscure pure impulse.[36]

Grotowski's signs are created anew out of the actor from "the
skeletal forms of human action, a crystallization of a role, an
articulation of the particular psycho-physiology of the actor."[37]
The signs result from the completeness of the specific actor's
surrender to his specific action and become a quintessential
expression of that actor's very existence. The eventual form of the
performance once developed, however, is as strictly composed as a
dogmatic religious ritual. Grotowski even speaks of the performance as a kind of *mask*; paradoxically, it is the mask of the
performance, the specific "system of signs" which, when performed totally by the actor, becomes the mechanism of the actor's
self-revelation. Like the ancient worshiper, then, Grotowski's
actor *authenticates and actually reveals his own existence through his skill as a
wearer of masks.*

Grotowski believes that the spectator, as Artaud had suggested,
imitates the actor's gesture and finds the same sort of spiritual
condition thereby excited in him. He disagrees with Artaud,
however, on the degree of effect thus achieved: Artaud believed
that the experience could be so massive and immediate that the
actor's performance could, by its intensity, crack the veneer of
civilized behavior almost at once; Grotowski more reasonably
understands that the full experience is inaccessible to the spectator
since it is, after all, the product of a long and rigorous training
experience to which the actor has totally dedicated himself. The

---

[35] *Ibid.*, pp. 17-18.
[36] *Ibid.*, p. 18.
[37] *Ibid.*, p. 24.

spectator must accept his share of the responsibility to work toward such a state and is encouraged in this by seeing what the actor has done as a kind of challenge:

> We are concerned with the spectator who has genuine spiritual needs and who really wishes, through confrontation with the performance, to analyze himself. . . . Each challenge from the actor, each of his magical acts (which the audience is incapable of reproducing) becomes something great, something extraordinary, something close to ecstasy.[38]

While the spectator is "incapable of reproducing" in any complete way the "magical acts" of the actor, Grotowski nevertheless believes he will receive an experience similar to that of the actor, though of reduced intensity:

> The member of an audience who accepts the actor's invitation and to a certain extent follows his example by activating himself in the same way, leaves the theatre in a greater state of inner harmony. But he who fights to keep his mask of lies intact at all costs, leaves the performance even more confused. I am convinced that on the whole, even in the latter case, the performance represents a form of social psychotherapy. . . .[39]

The actor's sacrifice merely points the way: there is no instant sainthood in Grotowski's theatre for the spectator nor, least of all, for the actor who takes upon himself a nearly monastic discipline.[40]

[38] *Ibid.*, pp. 40-41.
[39] *Ibid.*, p. 46.
[40] At the time of this writing, Grotowski has apparently undergone personal experiences of great magnitude, resulting in his moving toward an entirely new form of theatre involving celebratory festivals committed by nonprofessionals.

Ritual without Masks: The Living Theatre

No experimental theatre in our century has had as long or as varied a life as the Living Theatre under the leadership of Julian Beck and Judith Malina. Until they discontinued full-time performing in the spring of 1970 and broke into a number of smaller groups (including a communal core under the leadership of the Becks which is still performing), they had been in continuous existence for over twenty years and had spawned over forty "off-shoot" theatre groups. Although The Living Theatre began with an emphasis on poetic drama and a richly varied production history of established texts and distinguished adaptations, they metamorphosed through a series of milestone productions (e.g., *The Connection*, and *The Brig*) into an activist, anarchistic tribe which transcended the form of theatre altogether.

In their later work, especially *Frankenstein*, *Mysteries and Smaller Pieces* and the famous *Paradise Now*, they dispensed altogether with characterization and representation and attempted to create a kind of acting in which the actor discarded his mask and appeared entirely in his own persona. This kind of maskless acting is described by Saul Gottlieb, a member of the troupe, in a discussion with Dean Robert Brustein at the Yale Drama School:

> GOTTLIEB: . . . just in terms of experience, what the actor goes through in the plague scene of *Mysteries*—and I've acted it many times—is not illusionary. You go through a very real experience. . . . It's something that's very much involved with the reality of the person who is acting in his own life and with

the reality of the world in which we live and with the community of the audience.

BRUSTEIN: Stanislavski says exactly the same thing. Stanislavski wants you to return to the reality of the person who is creating the role. But you are always creating a role! Let's not forget that.

GOTTLIEB: Well, that's the difference—that we're not creating a role. We are becoming a part of ourselves, we are developing a part of ourselves when we do this.[41]

This sense of maskless acting was most highly developed in *Paradise Now* which was prepared, as Julian Beck explains to Richard Schechner, to avoid representational acting entirely:

> We said in preparing *Paradise Now* that we wanted to make a play which would no longer be enactment but would be the act itself, that we would not reproduce something but we would always ourselves be experiencing it, not anew at all but something else each time; not reproducing and bringing to life the same thing again and again and again but always it would be a new experience for us and it would be different from what we called acting.[42]

This desire to avoid enactment and instead "create an event," each performance of which would be a "new experience" for the actors and spectators, led the Living Theatre to a special kind of structure. They needed a form which could provide parameters within the limits of which the theatrical event could be created mutually by performers and spectators, but without the total loss of a sense of shape and direction. The form which evolved from their rehearsals for *Paradise Now* was a series of thematic segments based on the ten rungs of Martin Buber's Hassidic ladder; some of these segments were rehearsed and performed by the actors, while others were improvised around a theme or image by the actors and/or the audience. The whole was a game situation within whose outline a primary, nonmimetic event could be generated. As Julian Beck put it:

> What does it say at the bottom of the *Paradise Now* program? It says this chart is a map; we had

[41]"The Last Discussion," *Yale/Theatre* 2, no. 1 (Spring 1969): pp. 50-51.
[42]"Containment is the Enemy," *The Drama Review* 13, no. 3 (T43: Spring 1969): pp. 24-25.

originally intended to make a map that we would
be able to read in our own way for the night.[43]

Such a format can be broadly categorized in the same way as
Grotowski's structure, as a *ritual*, a sequence of activities which
move the celebrants through progressive states of consciousness
toward a spiritual catharsis.

Other avant-garde theatres have been attracted to the ritual
format although most (and particularly Grotowski and Joseph
Chaikin's Open Theater) have maintained a more specific and
rehearsed form than that used in *Paradise Now*. This general
tendency toward ritual in the experimental theatre is beautifully
summed up by Jean-Claude van Itallie in his preface to *The Serpent*, a
ritual performance developed by The Open Theater:

> Theatre is not electronic. Unlike movies and
> unlike television, it does require the live presence
> of both audience and actors in a single space. This
> is the theatre's uniquely important advantage and
> function, it's original religious function of
> bringing people together in a community
> ceremony where the actors are in some sense
> priests or celebrants, and the audience is drawn to
> participate with the actors in a kind of eucharist.[44]

This definition of the actor as a priest or celebrant, inspired by a
sense of a more primitive and vital era in the theatre's dim past, is
the fullest expression of acting as a state of *being* rather than one of
seeming. The actor-priest heightens and affirms his own existence
through the ceremony of the play; if the ceremony is to have its
effect, the audience must reciprocate, must in its turn affirm its
own role as co-celebrant in the ceremony. This sense of creative
participation by the audience was, as we have seen, common to
Meyerhold, Artaud, Grotowski and others; the great question,
however, is the form which this participation ought to take.
Grotowski believed that the audience could emulate the actor's
condition to some degree, but not directly join in it; the Living
Theatre insisted instead upon some form of active participation by
the spectator (or an overt refusal of participation, which they
considered an equally expressive act). For this reason, roughly
two-thirds of the ritual form of *Paradise Now* was purposely left

---

[43] *Ibid.*
[44] *The Serpent* (New York: Atheneum, 1970), p. ix.

open and unspecified in order to encourage and even force such active participation by the audience.

During these unrehearsed segments, the actors of the Living Theatre had no plot, no characterizations, "nothing but ourselves"; they confronted the audience in their own persons and pursued whatever events (or nonevents) the confrontation generated. Where actors in the past had accepted the form demanded by the role-mask, the actors of the Living Theatre used the occasion of the performance itself as a context for a realization of their own persons in a new dimension and as an occasion for a "real" event; they spent a good deal of time, for instance, watching the audience perform so that they became spectators as readily as their spectators could become performers. It was all a matter of really *being* there, really *doing* or *allowing* the event to occur. As Julian Beck put it in his notes on *Paradise Now*:

> The Form.
>> The Acting Form as The Form.
>> The Acting Form as The Mise-en-Scène.
>> State-of-Being Acting as opposed to
>> Enactment Acting.[45]

Or, as it was put in the discussion quoted earlier:

> BRUSTEIN: But, Saul, you are creating the role of yourself, you're still playing a role. And despite the fact that you do it on cue, when you're supposed to do it, in a theatre or outside it, it's no less a role.

> GOTTLIEB: You're being the role of yourself. We all have roles. . . . You're presenting your real self, as real as you can get, as close as you can get to your authentic self.[46]

The difference between the presentation of the actor's authentic, personal self within the performance expressed here and the sense of "uncovering" espoused by Grotowski is a crucial one: for Grotowski, the adoption of the mask of the performed character and the specific form of the performed ritual was the *process whereby the actor revealed himself*; the Living Theatre discarded the external mask of character altogether and presented instead the actor's individual and tribal self *directly* as both *the material and the form of the performance.*

[45]"Paradise Now: Notes," *The Drama Review* 13, no. 3 (T43: Spring 1969): p. 91.
[46]"The Last Discussion," *Yale/Theatre* 2, no. 1 (Spring 1969): p. 51.

As Dean Brustein pointed out, even such an actor is not truly maskless; none of us are truly maskless since the social personality is itself a kind of mask. But for the Living Theatre the *theatrical* persona was based entirely upon the actor's *social* persona, itself artistically heightened. In such a theatre, the actor had to commit his whole life and every shred of his energy to extending his expressive potential and his artistic and social thought; in short, he had to turn *himself* into an instrument of the theatre and his *life* into a dramatic occasion. Such a commitment was a deeply personal decision involved as much with politics and social values as with art.

The resultant performance was offered not as a representation of character but rather as an example and challenge to the spectator's own habitual mask. Through the confrontation, the spectator was dared to do what the actor had done and to make *of his life* an artistic creation. Julian Beck says in his notes:

> When the participants, mis-named the audience,
> all become the heroes in life that the actor is in
> his art, and when the actor takes the same trip in
> life that he does in his art, then we zoom into the
> next change, and it all begins to happen.[47]

Ironically, it is probably true that the Living Theatre, by discarding the aesthetic mask in favor of an artistic heightening of their own everyday social mask, sacrificed much of the capacity of the process of mask-wearing to move their audiences into extended, heightened or new states of reality. By de-emphasizing transformation into a new form and stressing instead self-realization, they deprived themselves and us of the very mechanism which could most help us to extend or alter our condition. Though the mask may temporarily obscure the wearer, the level of experience to which it may transport him cannot be attained without it. Discarding the mask altogether is a final act; it connotes the end of change, the end of the process of transformation which gives life its dynamism.

In short, if the actor permanently surrenders his mask in order to reveal himself, he surrenders also the mechanism whereby he may discover who he may become; state-of-being acting is therefore dramatically and spiritually inferior to acting-as-a-process-of-becoming.

[47] "Meditations: On the Life of Theatre," *Yale/Theatre* 2, no. 1 (Spring, 1969): p. 121.

Seeming, Being and Becoming

Nevertheless, no theatrical group in history has attained their own goals with the integrity and completeness of the Living Theatre, and no group has so permanently altered our perception of theatre. By transcending the theatre altogether, the Living Theatre entered completely into a state of *being* and renounced completely any trace of *seeming*. One reviewer accurately said that reviewing *Paradise Now* was much like reporting on a bus accident; it was a completely *primary* event. Despite my own disagreement with their form, I must report that no theatre experience in my life has taught me as much about myself, about my fellow spectators and about the theatre as did *Paradise Now*.

Beyond

The live theatre has the enormous variety of all human enterprise, ranging from complex organizations involving hundreds of workers reaching an audience of millions, to a handful of people performing in an abandoned warehouse before a group of spectators whom they may outnumber. The purposes of these theatres, regardless of their size, range from religious enlightenment and political reformation to cheap sensationalism. It is all theatre, just as we are all human beings, and judgment is rarely easy to pass.

This second part of the discussion has traced the development of only one dimension of acting, its spiritual aspect, in our own century. If much of the total variety of theatre has been omitted, it has not been because of a lack of respect for other theatrical forms on my part; rather, the concept of the spiritual or, in Grotowski's sense, *holy* actor seems to me one of growing importance in a broad variety of theatre and has special implications for the future of the art.

The development of this sense of spiritual acting has been indicated here by a survey of representative figures. Many more, known and unknown, would have to be included in any full accounting of acting in our time; in America I must pay special homage to Joseph Chaikin and The Open Theater (recently disbanded) and to Richard Schechner and The Performance Group. Each of these groups deserve chapters of their own, but luckily each is already well represented by the writings of their directors. Each of the figures I have surveyed, however, did contribute significantly to the general movement of acting away from mere representation and toward the creation of independent reality on the stage; that is, away from *seeming* and into *being*.

As we have seen, each contributed in his own way: the impulse toward *being* came out of naturalism and was given a spiritual dimension by Stanislavski, who remains the fountainhead of contemporary acting; the spirit of community which naturalism had unfortunately removed from the theatrical experience was restored by Meyerhold, who also gave us a renewed respect for the physicalities of performance; Brecht awakened our theatrical conscience; Artaud restored the irrational as the proper mode of the theatre; Grotowski showed that it is possible to synthesize these influences in a coherent and stable form; the Living Theatre attempted to bring the theatre directly and immediately into the daily consciousness of contemporary man.

Each of these and many other theatre artists working in our century have helped to restore our theatre to its ancient spiritual potential. The once degraded art of the actor is being made moral again in the deepest, most human sense of that word. Young theatre artists are returning to ancient impulses not to destroy current conventions, but to forge their own ideas, to drink, as it were, from the original well.

Just as this growing spirituality of the actor has been manifested in a broad variety of present theatrical practice, so the future will continue to display this same diversity of form. The young actor is privileged to look forward to a theatre of such variety and multiplicity of forms that virtually any taste or talent will be potentially capable of fulfillment; no longer shall a dominant style dictate which kind of acting will have the greatest chance of "success." The young theatre artist can seriously think about creating a theatre *in his own image*.

Most importantly, he can hopefully look forward to a life in the theatre motivated by meaningful moral or social purpose, a life in a deeply ethical profession of immediate importance to his culture.

This new freedom and purpose is not achieved cheaply, however. The older actor has the advantage of a relatively stable theatre premised upon a clear set of technical and aesthetic values which gave shape and direction to his training and development. Today's actor finds his theatre in such a state of disarray that he must exercise, along with all the fundamental disciplines of the actor, the additional self-discipline needed to form his own aesthetic vision and moral objectives. He must then pursue the agonizing search for the practical techniques which will bring his vision to fruition.

These are heavy dues, but the young artist willing to pay them will be repaid with a measure of artistic freedom and a sense of personal dignity unique in the entire history of our theatre.

It is a wonderful time to be an actor.

Part Three
Leaves, Flowers and Seeds

Leaves put to use the root's nourishment
And move with the wind and sun
Flowers attract and seduce
Seeds are the most hopeful parts of a plant

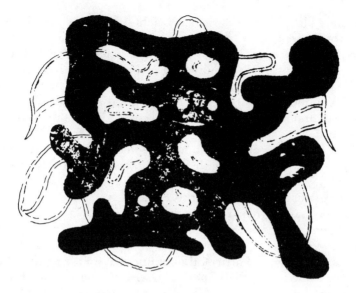

Seeming, being, becoming: three aspects of the actor's art which continually intermingle in the work of all actors, but which also have separate traditions and implications.

The traditional view of acting is one of *seeming*, of *representation*. The actor creates a character, but he is not that character; in the conventions of illusionistic theatre we willingly accept what the actor only seems to be *as if* it were real. This is the dominant, and the oldest, form of acting. Most of our greatest actors, whatever their individual methods of work, fall into this category, and our theatre is by and large still one of illusion, one of *seeming*.

But in the twentieth century, and specifically since Stanislavski, a significant number of actors have in some degree worked away from a theatre of seeming and toward a theatre of *being*. In a theatre of being, the separation of actor and character is reduced as much as possible, so that such an actor might say (as one did) "Play Lear? Hell, I *was* Lear!" At the other extreme, we have seen how some contemporary groups present the maskless actor in his own person ("Play Lear? Hell, I'm *me*!").

Such actors wish not merely to seem, but actually to *be*. In the past we have assumed that this desire for actuality on the stage was born out of the need to perform highly realistic plays in which the mere illusion of life was insufficient. It now appears, however, that the desire for actuality on the stage came from a much deeper impulse, an impulse that was observable in all the arts in the first half of this century. It is, moreover, an impulse which continues to motivate today's theatre and will continue to motivate the theatre of the immediate future, even though the forms which this impulse first took (that is, naturalism and realism) have been discarded.

That impulse is difficult to describe in words, but I will try: all art is a way of coping with mortality; when the artist creates something which is true, he has affirmed his own existence, he has participated somewhat in destiny.

I am not saying that art is simply a way of "beating" mortality, of feeling immortal, for that is a selfish and unrealistic motive. Art is not an evasion of mortality; rather, it is an act of celebration, of joyous acceptance, of affirmation of our place in the natural order. It is the same feeling that Spinoza described when he said that the acceptance of God permits the believer to participate in God; it was the feeling that the first masked dancer felt when he put on his mask and felt himself transported into a new plane of consciousness and existence. It is to feel bigger than yourself, to transcend the boundaries of individual existence. It is summed up best of all in the ancient and mysterious phrase, *yea-saying*.

It is not limited to art, of course. There is much of it in the deepest aspects of loving, of devotion and of child-rearing. Some find it even in the pursuit of a vocation. But the artist compacts this impulse to celebrate his existence into specific acts which may be recognizable to other men. He is, through his acts of creation, a way-shower first of all for himself, and therefore for others.

The actor is the most fortunate of all artists, for he participates most fully in his own act of celebration, he *is* his own art. The other arts provide the artist with some mechanism (paint, sound and so forth) with which he creates. The dancer and the actor, however, carry their art and its materials in their own spiritual and biological existence.

That is why for many actors a theatre of *seeming* was not enough; they wanted a theatre of *being* because only it allowed the fullest possible participation in the act of creative celebration.

But the form which this impulse to *be* took in the naturalistic and realistic theatres did not suit many and has, generally, left this impulse unsatisfied. Many actors, even at the beginning of this century, were searching for alternatives to naturalism, but *out of the same impulse.*

The father of the theatre of being, Stanislavski, manifested his sense of being as the actor's subjective experience. His philosophical opposite, Meyerhold, the father of the "plastic" or sculptural theatre and the theatre of signs (from which Artaud and Grotowski spring), manifested his sense of being in the experience which the theatre *per se* excited in the spectator. As opposed as their forms may appear, Stanislavski and Meyerhold were motivated by the same impulse toward *being.*

Even Brecht, whose theories mislead some into thinking that he espoused a theatre of *seeming,* was actually in search of the form which more truly allowed the actor to *be* in his *own* reality, a theatrical reality. Stanislavski exalted the reality of the character and wanted the actor to *be* totally in that reality; Meyerhold and Brecht were willing to modify the character's reality in order to allow the actor and his theatre to *be* more completely in their own actual selves, rather than in their illusory form.

Because all these men were working from a common motivation, today's theatre is able to draw freely on their ideas and to synthesize their merely apparent disagreements into entirely new forms of yea-saying, forms which have already been partially realized in the work of Jerzy Grotowski, Joseph Chaikin, Richard Schechner, Peter Brook and others.

Some of these same men, along with a few groups scattered throughout the world, have now begun to move beyond a theatre of being toward a new performance condition for the actor. I shall call this new condition a theatre of *becoming,* which I will attempt to describe here, although it defies verbal description. In any case, it is with us, and will soon reveal itself, in unexpected ways to be sure.

Becoming

We confront the actor in an uncapturable, unrepeatable moment in time when his mortality, heightened and clarified by his art, confronts our own. This human encounter will increasingly be the basis for our theatre in years to come. Thus the theatre of the immediate future will be neither a theatre of seeming, nor one of being, but one of *becoming*, a theatre celebrating the process of life itself. The actor of this theatre will, in his performance, constantly realize his own great weight in existence lying like a stone on the thin membrane of his mortality; he will be constantly defining himself through the dramatic act.

Drama must occur in the present
for only the present is always
and the only
true point of suspense.

The present is
a process of formation

By which form is given
to the limitless energy of the
    future

And the lifeless hulks of the
    known
drift into memory.

Drama is concerned with man's
    influence on
and subjectivity to
this process of becoming.

All art is generated by a fundamental aesthetic conflict between form and impulse, between the containment and the release of energy, between something coming to be and something ceasing to be.

Painting and sculpture are concerned with this conflict as it is manifested in line, mass, texture, color, figure and ground. Music realizes it in tonality, silence and time. Drama realizes it in the actions of men.

Each play expresses the fundamental aesthetic conflict in some specific way so as to illuminate the human condition. Each play focuses upon some specific aspect of man's attempt to deal with the flow of time.

The deepest vitality of the play flows from this profound stratum. Dramatic action, therefore, must touch an ancient part of us, must deal with survival—that is, with existence through time.

In the beginning there was the act . . . we have enough words . . . we are looking for acts.
—Jerzy Grotowski

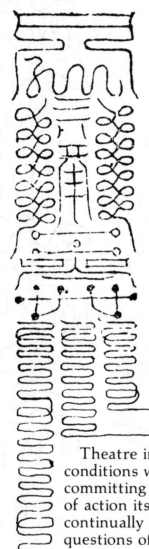

All plays occur in the present, the events happening not "as if" but actually "before our eyes." The tone of each play is much determined by the way it orients itself to the flow of time; standing in the present it may either greet the future or honor the past.

In the comedic posture man eagerly embraces the oncoming moment, saying his incessant "hello."

Tragedy lingers at the threshold of the past and lets us say our incessant "goodbye."

Tragedy is autumn passing into winter.

Goodbye.

Comedy is spring and the promise of summer.

Hello.

Theatre investigates the conditions which influence the committing of actions, the process of action itself, and therefore is continually involved with questions of existence, since action is the means whereby existence becomes self-defining.

Thoughts after a lecture on creativity
by psychoanalyst Rollo May

Creativity is the act of re-patterning the known world into meaningful new configurations. Man is a pattern-making animal; he no sooner confronts chaos than it dissolves into a projected pattern, usually a familiar one. In order to discover new patterns, the artist must at least momentarily divest himself of his habitual ways of seeing the world; as Don Juan puts it, he must "stop the world." Our habitual ways of seeing are in fact our *self*, an operative expression of who we are. Therefore, the artist must surrender his self in the act of creation in order to confront the chaos from which a new pattern may emerge. For this reason, Rollo May calls the creative act a form of psychological dying which must precede the rebirth expressed in the created form. Thus creativity is essentially an ongoing process of self-definition and extension for the artist. *Authentic* means "to be the author of yourself" so that the authentic person is involved in an ongoing creative process whether it has the form of a traditional "art" or not.

No artist has a greater opportunity for self-authorship than the actor.

The actor's mode of self-authorship is dramatic action, through which he allows his personal energies to flow into new configurations of the self. In this way, that which is essentially creative about acting is identical to that which is creative in everyday life.

Acting is not self-expression; it is self-extension.

Acting is neither seeming nor being; it is becoming.

The actor in a state of becoming is authentic. He continually dies in order to be continually reborn.

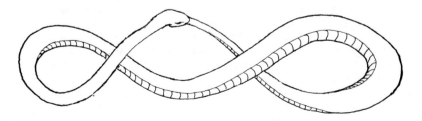

A performance is an organism
  which,
like any organism,
is continuously dying and being
  reborn.
It may pass a crisis
when the dying overtakes the
  borning
as it is said we all do.

This is the eternal origin of art: that a human being confronts a form that wants to become a work through him. Not a figment of his soul but something that appears to the soul and demands the soul's creative power. What is required is a deed that a man does with his whole being: if he commits it and speaks with his being to the form that appears, then the creative power is released and the work comes into being.

The deed involves a sacrifice and a risk. The sacrifice: infinite possibility is surrendered on the altar of the form . . . The risk: the basic work can only be spoken with one's whole being; whoever commits himself may not hold back part of himself . . . it is imperious: if I do not serve it properly, it breaks, or it breaks me.

—Martin Buber, *I and Thou*

We stand in the present and our view backward is as distorted as our view forward is conjectural. The telling of the future is, like the telling of the past, an act of interpretation, a selection of alternatives. Unlike the social or political historian, the artist finds the future more attractive than the past; the past has form, its circumstances are essentially beyond control. The past can be known but not met. But the future is suspenseful; it can be met but not known. Creative happiness comes from man's participation, through his art, in the meeting of the future, in his destiny. In his art, man can truly "get on with it."

Truth, for an actor, cannot exist *a priori* or even continue existing the moment after it comes to be; the actor's truth is in the act of unfolding the infinite present, in showing the inherent drama of our existence.

The sense of drama derives from the shaping of experience along the continuum of the present, the realization that we are in a state of continual expectation and that human interaction and emotion are mechanisms and manifestations of our incessant and dramatic encounter with the next moment.

Observe your reaction at a movie or play. Notice how, unaware, you identify with the characters. With which characters? Are there characters with whom you find it hard to identify?

Ability to evoke such identifications from the audience is crucial to an artwork's success in establishing its "reality"—that is to say, its illusion of reality. Popularity of the work stems largely from this. Yet works of art which accomplish only this have no great value, for it is a cheap experience (in no sense a recreation) to drain off emotions by habitual channels, whether real or fantasied. An art-experience is worth your while only if it leads you to a difficult identification, some possibility in yourself different from what is customary in action or wish—a larger vision or a subtler analysis. Furthermore, since from the standpoint of the serious artist, the handling, style and technique is of highest importance, remember that you cannot grasp this by simply sinking into the characters but only by concentrating on *how* they are being created. As you become aware of the style along with your awareness of the characters and plot, you will be identifying with the artist and will share something of his joy of creation.

—Frederick Perls, Ralph Hefferline,
and Paul Goodman, *Gestalt Therapy*.

No mechanism conceivable, no material we know of, is capable of the infinite variety and subtlety of the human organism.

Nothing can speak as directly or as deeply to us as one of us.

When the actor confronts the form that wants to become a work through him and commits himself to it with his whole being inspite of all sacrifice and risk, he becomes the art form, he *is* the art object in the process of becoming.

Nothing can speak as directly to us as one of us.

Nothing can speak as deeply to us as one of us.

The everyday man
    is what he does.
The actor also
    becomes whom he may be by doing.
We the watchers
    may also become
By joining our doing
    to the actor's doing:
Not as substitutes
    but as sharers
Who complete the chain of creation
    by allowing the force of the committed moment
    to resonate in us.
Lending to it our personal quality
    as the actor has lent his.

The most important aspect of the new theatre is our renewed sense of the requisite wholeness of the actor's self, and hence the breadth of his necessary discipline. . . .

We know that kinetic and kinesthetic deprivation in infancy inhibits personality development. The social persona is rehearsed in our first years largely through kinetic experience; it stands to reason that the dramatic persona is best rehearsed in the same way. Every actor knows that the work has not really begun until he gets up on his feet. It is only then, with script out of hand, in spatial and dynamic relationship with his partners and his environment, experiencing the transference of energy through their mutual pursuit of dramatic action, that their roles really begin to grow. Even Stanislavski, that great creator of "psycho-technique," was led in his last work to an emphasis on physical images and experience as the best inroads to the actor's total organism.

Moreover, the dramatic persona itself (we can't really go on speaking of "character" nowadays) is not only communicated to an audience through sensation but may actually be said to consist of a *mask of actions*, a pattern of organismic activity upon which the audience is led to project a full sense of identity, a pattern of organismic behavior in which both audience *and* actor participate and which is capable of generating a profound impact on the personality of both.

It is an idea fundamental to Artaud and Grotowski, but which needn't necessarily lead one in their directions.

From all this it seems an inescapable conclusion that movement training in the broadest sense (and thus encompassing vocal training) is the most important single aspect of a young actor's development. Every serious training program that I know of has come or is coming to this realization.

Grotowski says that "we are entering the age of Artaud." I say that we are entering the age of Meyerhold.

"Illusion," as it was once called in the theatre, is a matter of encouraging the audience to re-interpret their (and our) reality. The strength of the re-interpretation depends entirely on the strength and fullness of our performance reality.

The performance reality is one of real organisms in real space, expressing real energies in real conflict.

The actor who ignores performance reality is lost.

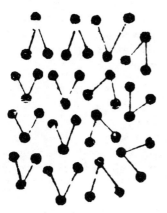

An actor's weight is
His principal reality.
He feels it
In the soles of his feet,
In every inclination,
Rotation,
Change in altitude
In every motion
At every moment.
There is no relationship
Where weight is not given
And taken.

Freedom of conception for the actor must include free disposition of his weight. Karate, tumbling, Tai Chi and the rest can liberate the actor by extending his range of choice. Imagine yourself onstage, knowing that you could, if you chose, leap into the air and flip over. This possibility so alters your range of choice that hosts of new possibilities, physical and spiritual, come easily into view.

Have you ever caught yourself putting the "best" books in a prominent place on the shelf? We know that others read our character from the context we have created; in real life, then, character is communicated not only through the presentation of self but also through *the manipulation of context.*

So too, the stage actor is concerned not only with a performance which is a set of actions, but also with the creation of a context within which those actions are interpreted. For this reason the actor's job has never been merely the creation of his own charac- ter; all the members of a cast must share in the responsibility of creating a total context of maximum value to each performance.

This is done primarily through *relationship,* the way each actor/ character relates to every other actor/character; we must support each other's identity by creating a totally supportive context in which those identities will be interpreted.

In short, it is untrue to think of an actor creating *his* character; each actor's character is created by all the actors. In fact, *actors create each other's characters on stage more than they create their own.*

That is why the group, the ensemble, is today such an essential aspect of live theatre; that is why the solo, star performer or virtuoso has so little place in the new theatre.

And it is the absence of the opportunity for intimate ensemble playing and the reliance on merely individual creativity that produces so much mediocre acting in film and television.

The work makes the group
The group does not make the work

A good team member needs to be an expert
at saying goodbye
The moment he *needs* the group
he has become dangerous

Group membership must enhance the individual identity of each member,
He must get more than he gives
Or he will
in his heart of hearts
come to hate it
and will conspire unconsciously for its destruction.

The work makes the group
The group does not make the work

A group chooses to be at every moment
out of artistic necessity
And every member works with every other
out of mutual respect for the shared vision
and out of respect for the talents of every other
and for his own talent
People in groups need time away
time alone
time with other groups
time with others
Remember:

If I know how to be alone
I can be more with you.

No one tells the painter how it should look
No one tells the composer how it should sound
No one tells the writer what it should say
But an agent
Who has never acted in his life
Tells me to cut off my beard.

Do we expect to listen to the symphony
                                        once
Do we expect to see the painting
                                        once
Must we make do with one sip of the fine
wine and say, yes I had that
                                        once
But the play? Oh, I saw that one.
                                        once

Kleenex.

The greatest child actor in the Peking Opera
is seventy-five years old.
But I have to cut off my beard.

              It will not change;
              we will merely find a new home.

A Letter from a Young Actor Friend

We've got to stick together these days, we actors—or it will all slip away. I hope young actors will start their own journals; journals that contain their own feelings about their work with others and any pieces they may pick up through reading and working. Pieces that inside make a difference—perhaps to no one else.

Gotta tell you something and I hope you understand. Why do actors—other actors, myself—sometimes, a lot of times, feel embarrassed about working hard or baring parts of our emotional selves in the course of our work? Even older actors—even the most professionally secure actors—when a gamble or a stretch would help them to feel less isolated.

Safety is the watchword in so many cases: you know, don't put yourself out too far on the limb or you may appear stupid or put the other actors in an uncomfortable position. I know it sounds absurd but it happens—it happens and I can't stand it. I hope your book helps to encourage young actors away from this quicksand—make them feel special and able to do things that 99.9% of other people can't do.

Like tonight I was a Russian Cavalry Lieutenant and also a tenement dweller with a wife and kids freezing in Petersburg! I was! I traveled to a different world—two different worlds, really. I talked different, looked different, felt strange and new emotions—that was *special*; not just a job or an Equity contract of $172 a week for services rendered in two bit parts.

I just don't understand how actors can fall into the trap and miss what's special about it—but it happens. All the time. Especially when you perform every night and rehearse all day for a few months—for some, a few years. God, if it's not special, if its not coming from your guts and mind, if you're not stretching to find things—then why do it? Why waste your time putting on pancake and a frock coat and trip through the evening? Why waste the audience's time when they can go to the flicks and see them do it to perfection?

Sometimes I feel like most actors mean well and try to do their best—they get into it and really do it out in performance—but it's too late and they don't know it. Way back in rehearsal, maybe at the very first reading, they didn't care enough, didn't push themselves, didn't really dig. But why should they? It's a chain reaction; everyone follows the leader into safety. Nobody notices. Right? It happens.

And everyone wonders why the people don't want to come. Through no conscious fault of their own, the actors have nothing really happening; all the lighting effects and costumes and revolves won't help.

This is bothering me, Beny; I hope your book might help us actors (us migrants) to make an emotional home in any rehearsal hall or dressing room we enter and really get down to work without freaking everyone out! Maybe we'll start celebrating the fact that we're together in rehearsal rather than watching clock and playing poker—actors here ask for special pockets in their costumes to keep their poker money in! Good lord, what are they doing? Its like an absurd play.

But—you've got to eat and support yourself so you cool it and do your work—and take razz for spending two hours in front of the make up mirror preparing for a four-minute scene. But it matters to you, it's special, it's a celebration, it's your own party and that's OK. I don't like it, but that's how it goes—and sometimes you *do* find the guy or two who's grooving too—who really cares—and that's great.

And I'm learning and growing—and that's good. It's worth it.

It helps, I think, to consider ourselves on a very long journey: the main thing is to keep to the path, to endure, to help each other when we stumble or tire, to weep and press on. Perhaps if I had a coat of arms, this would be my motto: Weep and begin again . . .

Tears will make our flesh tender. A soft nest for mother-and-child. A soft stone nest for fledgling fire.

The art of non-resistance. One gives up the persona, as Yeats would say, and takes up the mask. That is to say, one becomes that which is not. Free where one is bound. The physics is clear. The way to center is by abandonment . . .

Am I willing to give up what I have in order to be what I am not yet? Am I willing to let my ideas of myself, or man, be changed? Am I able to follow the spirit of love into the desert? To empty myself even of my concept of emptiness? Love is not an attitude. It is a bodily act. In my crisis of conscience I have to yield myself to the transforming condition of love. It is a frightening and sacred moment. There is no return. One's life is changed forever. It is the fire that gives us our shape.

And yet, though everything is changed, everything remains still to do. Ordeal by fire is a lengthy labor. But at last we know ourselves under way. And though we may sweat and weep as much as before, we know that the make-believe life is over. We know that we labor upon the true vine that grows in us and that will one day bear its fruit. And as we labor together in this unfathomable vineyard, how fraternally we may cheer each other on in the common task. What could be better than that man's work should become the world's freedom, and man's enjoyment the world's perfecting?

—Mary Caroline Richards, *Centering*

For the actor
A role is a journey.
At any moment
He can only be
At that one point
To which his steps have led.

An ancient Chinese acting
manual defines acting as
*The art of standing still
while not standing still.*
—A. C. Scott

A sign of the understanding of things by the new actors is the great stillness at the center which so many of them bring to their work; time was when such a stillness was found only in older actors, in the Scofields and the Redgraves, and especially in very old actors, in the Gielguds and the Munis. It is a source of great strength and freedom of imagination, this stillness at the center. It comes from understanding things. It will make the theatre an even more valuable place in the years to come, a place where once again all may dip into the pool, and touch the stillness.

Picasso had a roomful of paintings which no one else had ever seen. Some weren't finished, some weren't good enough but were too good to destroy, and many were simply *his*.

Actors have such rooms in their minds full of unfinished performances and performances which are simply their own private property.

It is important to the actor, like the painter, to say to something which he has made, "I love you."

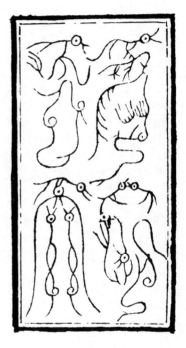

Jim has given himself to acting completely; it was a deliberate choice. Already he has begun to learn the everyday things that accumulate, building the mound of artistry; not monumental revelations, but little chips and sweepings that begin to fill the corners of the mind. Someday he will quietly be a man of the theatre looking back and being sure that he never really did his best; but the actor early learns to forgive himself for the inevitable incompleteness of his art, and this Jim has already learned.

Actors must at some time learn
to be more moved than moving.
When we open ourselves to the
energies of the play and let
them flow through us, we discover that every good play is
itself a source of vitality. The
good actor doesn't *make* things
happen, he *lets* things happen
and joins them.

Our roles in real life are in many ways as set as a dramatic
performance; the range of choices available to the actor in his
stage role is as great as those offered to him in his social role.

Within any form, no matter how narrow, there exists an infinity
of choice. As the specific demands of the form increase (as in
"stylized" performance) the *scale* of choice decreases, but the *range*
of choice does not.

Becoming in all kinds of performance is dependent on realizing
and experiencing this, and participating fully in the act of choice on
the largest scale of choice made available by the form.

A single breath offers such an infinity of possibilities.

The director's purpose is to
create a condition which leads
another (the actor) to a new
experience . . . a thousand times
it won't work, but once it will—
and that once is essential.
—Jerzy Grotowski in a talk at
New York University.

The director is the magnifying lens
    through which the actor's impulse shines;
The director is the resonator
    which lends depth to the actor's music.

The director must not use his actors
    as instruments to make
    his own music,
but orchestrate theirs
    until it becomes one song
    which he can then
    share in singing.

Beginning with Artaud in the thirties, there has been a feeling that theatre ought to get out from under the "dictatorship of speech." This anti-verbal feeling comes from a misunderstanding of the function and nature of language in life, which itself reflects one of the limitations of our culture.

We are bombarded by anonymous voices from the media and it often seems that the act of speech has ceased to be a physical and totally expressive act. We live in an age of the plastic voice. It has become a cultural norm, and in order to reproduce it in ourselves and our children we have begun to develop, unconsciously, inhibitions of the expressive processes of the body which produce speech. Rather than regard speech as an enemy to theatre, it should be one of the missions of the theatre to restore to our culture a sense of the real expressiveness and force of language.

Speech forms a kind of pointing and, more specifically, a kind of grasping. You can see this in babies; at a certain age they can reach out and grasp an object physically; at some point they discover that the voice can reach further than the arm. The word or sound becomes a way to possess, a kind of long-distance tasting. Language from the beginning has this physical basis as a way of extending the power of oneself through space. This sense of language as a force with which we can sculpt the space of the stage, with which we can create textures in the space of the stage, with which we can exert a real, physical influence on our environment, must be restored to the theatre.

*Some random predictions on theatre
in the year 2000*

The actor will use the same great range of skills that we see today in the Oriental actor: singing, dancing, pantomime, acrobatics, all synthesized into one organically whole mode of performance.

Lyrical (rather than "musical") **theatre** will be extended into forms which will fulfill the original impulses of opera before it was perverted by bel canto.

Related performance forms will be increasingly involved in theatre and will undergo revivals of their own; magic and the circus are two whose revivals have already begun.

Outdoor drama will continue to grow in popularity.

Agrarian theatre, free of the city, will be important.

Spectacle in the sense of lighting, costuming, sound effects, elaborate settings, will continue to decrease in importance.

Environmental staging will continue to grow in popularity and the proscenium arch will virtually disappear.

Large permanent companies with their elaborate plants will number only two or three on our continent.

Street theatre and theatre outside of traditional "theatres" will continue to grow.

Touring companies will be more numerous; there will probably be a revival of the great theatrical circuits.

Government subsidy will not proportionately increase, but large corporations will begin to support even experimental theatres.

Communities of theatre people (rather than "communes") will spring up in and out of the cities; with this will come a reawakened sense of involvement of theatre in its community.

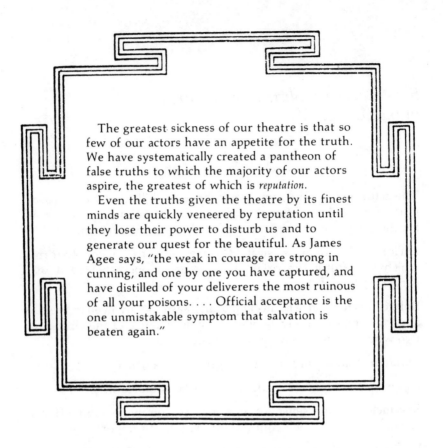

The greatest sickness of our theatre is that so few of our actors have an appetite for the truth. We have systematically created a pantheon of false truths to which the majority of our actors aspire, the greatest of which is *reputation*. Even the truths given the theatre by its finest minds are quickly veneered by reputation until they lose their power to disturb us and to generate our quest for the beautiful. As James Agee says, "the weak in courage are strong in cunning, and one by one you have captured, and have distilled of your deliverers the most ruinous of all your poisons. . . . Official acceptance is the one unmistakable symptom that salvation is beaten again."

Sadly, many teachers whose perceptions become "recognized" lose much of their potency, since their leadership is then sought for wrong reasons, and their thoughts accepted as rote methodology rather than as the living, often contradictory, and agonized struggle with fundamental aesthetic principles which they are.

To see that this is true you need only realize how much of Stanislavki's work has been "frozen" at some particular point of its development and is now taught as completed system. The overall direction of his entire life's search is little taken into account. As a result we fail to continue his work and instead have attempted to capture and endlessly repeat it. Thus we lose the potency of his perceptions which should be signposts in the path of our own search.

We are suggesting here a way of looking at the actor's function; we are not developing a system in the way that Stanislavski spoke of this "system." Techniques of analysis and systems of criticism are useful only insofar as they help to explore, extend, and clarify our aesthetic responses; they can never be a substitute for aesthetic response. When they begin to determine or predispose aesthetic response they must be destroyed. The same thing applies to an educational situation. The moment you let any teacher's system or way of seeing things begin to replace your own, that's no education in any sense of the word whatsoever. Anything that can be taught on that basis is really not worth learning.

When thinking about your work and the work of your teachers remember that the real effect of your training will never be immediately apparent, nor will you be able to recognize or evaluate those deepest effects for some time. This is why firm trust in your teachers is indispensible, even when it is unjustified.

On Regularity

I had a friend in Chicago who loved to get home in the evening and polish his shoes; it was the one job in the day, he said, that he could finish completely with his own hands. Writing, fashioning at least one living idea out of a pile of words each day, has come to serve me in the same way: it is more than a necessary discipline, even more than a habit; it has become a need, a way of working things out, of giving clear form and purpose to the often chaotic and always unfinished business of teaching young people to act.

Why, in our rich country, cannot more actors have the kinds of positions that would give them this satisfaction of daily labor at their craft? We hoped in the early Sixties that the fledging repertory theatres were going to provide such opportunities, but a decade later we find that only six or seven established companies have survived, providing perhaps three hundred stable yearly jobs among them. For the rest, the media industry offers a few days' work at a high daily rate; the commercial theatre offers a few roles a year at a moderate weekly salary; and between these days and these weeks are the months of foraging, the time away from growth; for these actors are forced to expend more energy in finding work than in developing their artistry.

If actors were deer, we would have to shoot most of the herd.

Many young actors have no wish to join the foraging fight and are beginning to band together in makeshift companies which, however modest, at least provide an opportunity for regular development. They say:

> We're tired of making *careers*
> We're tired even of making *shows*
> Let us begin to make *a theatre*.

But no one hears, not the foundations, not the government, not the patrons who spent the millions and millions on the half-empty dream of the last decade.

On Change

The established theatre
    whatever its qualities at any moment in time
    however base or exalted
    is an operative system.
The artist who is compelled otherwise
    than the established ways
Must abandon the system
    for the system ultimately reproduces
    only itself.

But the new wines in the new bottles
    are soon drunk
    soon faded
    soon spilled
By time, changing custom, changing values
    and the young who are their embodiment.
Theatre is, like all,
    an unending reciprocity
    between the stability and dignity of the inevitably old
    and the vigor of the irresistible young
    between what is and what will be.
Why do we not then invite change
    with greater gladness?
Why do we not then offer it
    with greater respect?

The real distinction between the "establishment" theatre and the avant-garde today is the difference between product and process. The commercial product is just that, a *product*, over, finished, dead.

It has ceased to change in any essential way, and in this universe arrested change is eventual death. No matter how long the rewrites go on (from Burrows to Albee to Chance), no matter how many changes are made during previews, the essential life of it was over and done with somewhere back in the producer's office.

The commercial product strives to give the impression that the actor is immortal, even plasticized, and that if he should crack and go bad, don't worry, we have 420 other actors waiting for the part with no noticeable change in the performance. Most of the actors working steadily in New York are replacements in long runs. They play the part of the actor who played the part of the actor who "created" the role.

By the time it gets to us it cannot hurt us. The actor's mortality, his spark of the vanished instant, has been captured and neutralized; he dies/lives in a life/death before us.

The avant-garde, the best of it, the part which isn't establishment theatre hiding under a foundation grant or academic robe, is a theatre of *process*. Whatever it may be telling you, it is also saying, "whoops, there it goes, that will never happen again."

And hopefully it helps you to realize that *you* will never happen again; whoops, there you go.

The Broadway season begins with the autumn and ends with the spring, catching the cycle of seasons in its turn through decay, but suspending during the summer months of growing maturity. May this help to explain the growing popularity of summer drama festivals as an alternative to the deadliness of the regular commercial season?

Each role, each production, gives specific motivation and direction to the work of the actor. Every show is everything to him, because it is at that moment his vehicle of self-authorship . . . but behind this obsession with THE SHOW is also a sense of ME becoming an actor . . . til death do us part.

The theatrical experience is inevitably one of process, not because we make it that way, but because it is the product of a confluence of life energies flowing through time; the audience and actors become a temporary tribe, dying and being reborn at each moment. What is therefore truly unique and transcendant about theatre is the possibility that the actor might drop dead.

A great deal of the theatre one sees today is not theatre at all, but staged critical essays. The ideas have been worked out perfectly, but the production has failed as a theatrical experience, and has remained an analytical experience.

Not that ideas are necessarily dull or destructive in the theatre—Shaw, Brecht and Ibsen wouldn't think so—but it matters whether the idea has generated a theatrical form, or whether the theatre has been merely used to support or communicate ideas. The theatre has risen up in the last two decades and said "I will not be used."

111

"Poetry," said Wallace Stevens, "is a process of the personality of the poet." Creative work is a training of each individual's perception according to the level on which he is alive and awake; that is why it is so difficult to evaluate. And it should be difficult. In art, perception is embodied: in dust, in pigment, in sounds, in movements of the body, in metals and stone, in threads and stuff. Each product, each goal, in an intermediate moment in a much longer journey of the person.

Incarnation: bodying forth. Is this not our whole concern? The bodying forth of our *sense of life?* . . . We body forth our ideals in personal acts, either alone or with others in society. We body forth felt experience in a poem's image and sound. We body forth our inner residence in the architecture of our homes and common buildings. We body forth our struggles and our revelations in the space of theatre. That is what form is: the bodying forth. . . .

The innerness of the so-called outer world is nowhere so evident as in the life of our body. The air we breathe one moment will be breathed by someone else the next and has been breathed by someone else before. We exist as respiring, pulsating organisms within a sea of life-serving beings. As we become able to hold this more and more steadily in our consciousness, we experience relatedness at an elemental level. We see that it is not a matter of trying to be related, but rather of living consciously into the actuality of being related. As we yield ourselves to the living presence of this relatedness, we find that life begins to possess an ease and a freedom and a naturalness that fill our hearts with joy. . . .

These thoughts are from a book called *Centering* by Mary Caroline Richards. She is a potter and a poet; as a potter, she knows how the centering of the clay upon the wheel is essential to creation, for only from perfectly centered clay can the motions of the wheel and of the potter's hands bring forth freely, naturally, the flow of the pot's shape toward its ultimate form. As a poet, she knows how the experiences of one's life must touch a personal center before they can in turn form outward, be bodied forth, in the form of a poem. We teachers of acting, and we actors, also know how the actor, in the deepest way, must center himself; as he touches his own center he, like the clay, is liberated to flow outward into new forms that are profoundly organic expressions of his transformed life energies.

112

The root of the matter is the way in which we feel and conceive ourselves as human beings, our sensation of being alive, of individual existence and identity. We suffer from a hallucination, from a false and distorted sensation of our own existence as living organisms. Most of us have the sensation that "I, myself" is a separate center of feeling and action, living inside and bounded by the physical body—a center which "confronts" an "external" world of people and things, making contact through the senses with a universe both alien and strange. Everyday figures of speech reflect this illusion. "I came into this world." "You must face reality." "The conquest of nature."

This feeling of being lonely and very temporary visitors in the universe is flat contradiction to everything known about man (and all other living organisms) in the sciences. We do not "come into" this world; we come *out* of it, as leaves from a tree. As the ocean "waves" the universe "peoples." Every individual is an expression of the whole realm of nature, a unique action of the total universe. This fact is rarely, if ever, experienced by most individuals. Even those who know it to be true in theory do not sense or feel it, but continue to be aware of themselves as isolated "egos" inside bags of skin.

—Alan Watts, *The Book*

There are, in the mountain tundra, vast fields of talus,
jumbled expanses of boulders of all sizes,
which lie threatening like the boilings of a gigantic caldron
frozen in stone. You may cross them in several ways:

As most do, clambering painfully on all fours like some
scuttling anachronism;

As some do, by climbing a large rock and charting a course,
leaping from point to point,
only to find that as their point of view shifts
the premeditated course must be continuously revised;

As the artist must, by joining the rock and finding at each step
only the next rock
and trusting the continuity of his own activity
to bring him to the other side.

Find the next step, even if it appears to lead in the wrong
direction; eventually the way will be found.

As you find the rhythm of the rock, you begin to run.

Work done in the mountains
    or in the forest
Is different from city work.

An actor, open as he must be to his place,
        his fellows,
Is played by his world
        like a violin.
The city plucks you
        and bows harshly
Producing perhaps greater volume
        and often a vivid melody,
But the mountains play you deep
        and long
In sustained chords
        and with a truer song.

Drama was in the beginning a celebration at least in part of
the rhythm of the land.
There is for us now
a desperate need to feel it again.

Gardening is an excellent discipline
for the actor's spirit
and conception.
An exercise:
   grow one plant from seed,
   to root
   to stem
   to branch
   to leaf
   to flower
   to autumn
   to death/birth
   to seed.
Identify each stage in the growth
of the actor's role.

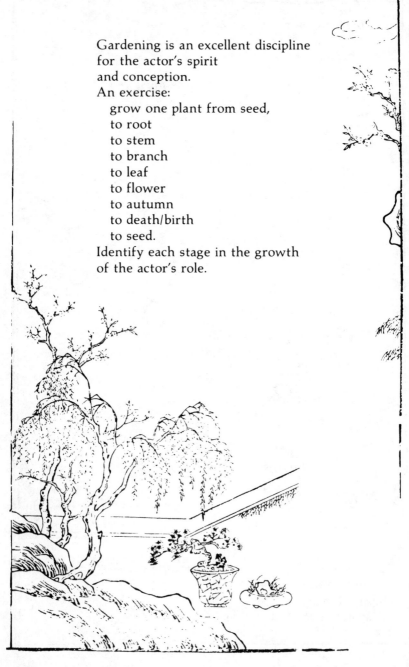

The Zen Buddhist
believes that the
gardener's job is to
extend nature in the
direction in which it is
already going. That is
what we must do when
we translate our truths
from everyday life into
the language of the
theatre. We must use
the theatre in such a
way as to take those
truths from life and
expand them in the
theatre in the direction
in which they are
already going.

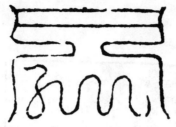

Comedy celebrates the ascendency of man over time
and tragedy his surrender to it.

                             Ripeness.

Comedy the promise of spring
Tragedy the ripeness of autumn.

                             Ripeness.

As the plant grows, so grows man;
comedy the sowing,
tragedy the reaping.

                         Ripeness is all.

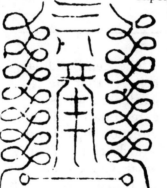

The actor has always known this in the rhythms of comedy
and tragedy,
in the direction of the force that drives through each.

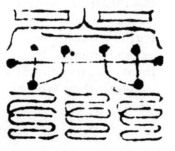

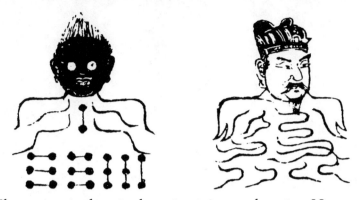

The man on the airplane is a neuro-chemist. He reveals that the oldest part of the brain, in its stem in the hollow at the top of the neck, is concerned with home-thermic responses—our impulse to find comfortable temperatures, and thus a major instrument of racial survival. The aesthetic response, we agree, ought to touch such a deep and ancient part of us; but have we ever fiddled with the temperatures of our theatres to do it? We are still seeking the optimum comfort in our art; when will we finally begin to disorder the very apparatus of survival for the sake of our art? We agree, but he is a 50-year-old Jew and he reminds me that Hitler succeeded thus in *his* art. But our art is not Hitler's; it is not an art of control and manipulation of response or thought, I say. The actor-fascist who enjoys manipulating his audience's minds and emotions is being replaced by a magician, by a giver of truth and delight. He hopes so. We fly on.

I believe that as a culture, we have lost control of objective reality and are desperate to gain control of subjective reality. The recent renaissance of religion, magic, circus, therapy, meditation — and theatre — expresses this need.

The actor cares
   but not for himself

The actor shares
   but does not exhibit

The actor loves
   but does not court

The actor receives
   but does not take

The actor's joy
   is in truth

See not who he is
   but who he has become

Bibliography

Archer, William. *Masks or Faces*. New York: Hill and Wang, 1957.

Artaud, Antonin. *The Theatre and Its Double*. New York: Grove Press, 1958.

Baumol, William J. and William G. Bowen. *Performing Arts: The Economic Dilemma*. New York: Twentieth Century Fund, 1966.

Beck, Julian. "Meditations: On the Life of Theatre," *Yale/Theatre* 2, no. 1 (1969): 117-127.

Benedetti, Robert L. *The Actor at Work*. rev. ed. Englewood Cliffs, N.J.: Prentice-Hall, 1976.

Braun, Edward, ed. and trans. *Meyerhold on Theatre*. New York: Hill and Wang, 1969.

Brockett, Oscar. *The Theatre: An Introduction*. New York: Holt, Rinehart, and Winston, 1964.

Brustein, Robert. "The Last Discussion," *Yale/Theatre* 2, no. 1 (1969): 45-52.

Buber, Martin. *I and Thou*. Translated by Walter Kaufmann. New York: Scribner's, 1970.

Campbell, Joseph. *The Masks of God: Primitive Mythology*. New York: Viking Press, 1959.

Cole, Toby and Helen Chinoy, ed. *Directors on Directing*. Indianapolis: Bobbs-Merrill, 1953.

Esslin, Martin. *Brecht: The Man and His Work*. Garden City, N.Y.: Doubleday, 1960.

Goffman, Erving. *The Presentation of Self in Everyday Life*. Garden City, N.Y.: Doubleday, 1959.

Green, Michael. *Downwind of Upstage*. New York: Hawthorn Books, 1964.

Grotowski, Jerzy. *Towards a Poor Theatre*. New York: Simon and Schuster, 1968.

Hapgood, Elizabeth Reynolds, ed. and trans. *Stanislavski: An Actor's Handbook*. New York: Theatre Arts Books, 1963.

The Living Theatre. *"Paradise Now:* Notes," *The Drama Review* 13, no. 3 (1969): 90-107.

Otto, Walter. *Dionysus: Myth and Cult*. Bloomington: Indiana University Press, 1965.

Perls, Frederick, Ralph Hefferline and Paul Goodman. *Gestalt Therapy*. New York: Julian Press, 1951.

Richards, Mary Caroline. *Centering: In Pottery, Poetry and the Person*. Middletown, Conn.: Wesleyan University Press, 1969.

Schechner, Richard. "Containment Is the Enemy; An Interview with the Becks," *The Drama Review* 13, no. 3 (1969): 24-44.

Shalleck, Jamie. *Masks*. New York: Viking Press, 1973.

Strindberg, August. "Notes to the Members of the Intimate Theatre," *Tulane Drama Review* 6 (1961).

van Itallie, Jean-Claude. *The Serpent.* New York: Atheneum, 1970.

Watts, Alan. *The Book: On the Taboo Against Knowing Who You Are.* New York: Collier Books, 1966.

Wilde, Oscar. *The Picture of Dorian Grey.* Harmondsworth, England: Penguin Books, 1963.

Willett, John, ed. and trans. *Brecht on Theatre.* New York: Hill and Wang, 1957.